Historical American Biographies

BENEDICT ARNOLD

Patriot or Traitor?

Ann Graham Gaines

 Enslow Publishers, Inc.

40 Industrial Road   PO Box 38
Box 398   Aldershot
Berkeley Heights, NJ 07922   Hants GU12 6BP
USA   UK
http://www.enslow.com

Library of Congress Cataloging-in-Publication Data

Gaines, Ann.
    Benedict Arnold : patriot or traitor? / Ann Graham Gaines.
        p. cm. — (Historical American biographies)
    Includes bibliographical references and index.
    Summary: Describes the life and times of Benedict Arnold, giving a
glimpse into the man whose name became synonymous with the word
"traitor."
    ISBN 0-7660-1393-6
    1. Arnold, Benedict, 1741–1801—Juvenile literature. 2. American
loyalists—Biography—Juvenile literature. 3. Generals—United States—
Biography—Juvenile literature. 4. United States. Continental Army—
Biography—Juvenile literature. 5. United States—History—Revolution,
1775–1783—Juvenile literature. [1. Arnold, Benedict, 1741–1801.
2. American loyalists. 3. Generals. 4. United States—History—
Revolution, 1775–1783—Biography.] I. Title. II. Series.

E278.A7 G35 2001
973.3'092—dc21
[B]
                                                        00-008732

Printed in the United States of America

10 9 8 7 6 5 4 3 2 1

To Our Readers: All Internet addresses in this book were active and appropriate
when we went to press. Any comments or suggestions can be sent by e-mail to
Comments@enslow.com or to the address on the back cover.

Illustration Credits: Enslow Publishers, Inc., pp. 18, 47, 49, 81, 106;
John Grafton, *The American Revolution: A Picture Sourcebook* (New
York: Dover Publications, Inc., 1975), pp. 38, 44, 55, 76, 88, 92, 95,
101; National Archives, pp. 11, 30, 34, 36, 115; Reproduced from the
Dictionary of American Portraits, Published by Dover Publications, Inc.,
in 1967, pp. 4, 41, 54, 61, 71, 77.

Cover Illustration: National Archives (Inset); Enslow Publishers, Inc.
(Background).

CONTENTS

Although he was a distinguished leader in the Revolutionary War,
Benedict Arnold is best known for being a traitor to his country.

1

THE BATTLE OF TICONDEROGA

B enedict Arnold, who later became so famous as a traitor, distinguished himself early in the American Revolution. After the Battles of Lexington and Concord on April 19, 1775, the first fighting of the revolution, thousands of colonists flocked to Boston, prepared to fight the British. Benedict Arnold was among the militiamen who rode there from New Haven, Connecticut. Within days, there were more than twenty thousand New Englanders surrounding the British forces in Boston.

There were plenty of men, but there was little else. This rag-tag army lacked food, blankets, uniforms, cannons, and leadership. The men needed someone to organize them into a disciplined army.

The Continental Congress, in which delegates represented every colony, had already been in existence for more than six months. However, the Continental Congress would not vote to recognize the American forces near Boston as the Continental Army and appoint George Washington its commander until June 1775.[1] Until then, the Massachusetts Committee of Safety, a group of Boston patriots, assumed control of the many different militias in Boston.

Benedict Arnold realized that, unless the rebels who had gathered in Boston got some artillery, they had no hope of driving away the British. He also knew where there were many cannons with little or no British protection.

As a merchant, Arnold had often traveled to Canada to buy and sell merchandise. A few years earlier, Canada had belonged to France. The French had built Fort Ticonderoga, a strong fortification near the southern tip of Lake Champlain, to help defend Canada against a British invasion. In the 1750s, during the French and Indian War, the British attacked Fort Ticonderoga several times. The British finally won the war—and all of Canada. Fort Ticonderoga, in the middle of British territory, was abandoned by the French. It was allowed to deteriorate and crumble. However, Arnold knew from his recent travels to Canada that there were still more than eighty cannons at Fort Ticonderoga, protected by only forty-six British soldiers. He realized that even a few patriots—acting quickly and using the element of surprise—could seize these cannons for the use of the American forces.[2]

Arnold and his militia reached the patriot headquarters at Cambridge, Massachusetts, on April 29, 1775. The very next day, he went to explain his idea for seizing Ticonderoga to the Massachusetts Committee of Safety. Its members asked him to submit a written proposal for the attack on the fort. On May 2, the committee made Arnold a colonel in the Massachusetts militia. It also authorized him to recruit up to four hundred men for the expedition.[3] The committee gave him one hundred pounds (the money used in America at the time), ten horses, two hundred pounds of gunpowder, two hundred

Fort Ticonderoga

Fort Ticonderoga, first built by the French, was located at the southern tip of Lake Champlain in what is now New York State. Its location made Ticonderoga strategically important. It controlled what activity could take place on Lake Champlain and the Hudson River. The Americans wanted to seize Ticonderoga. If they did so, they could regulate communications between Canada and the colonies, preventing British soldiers and supplies from being easily sent across the border.

pounds of lead balls, and a thousand flints, and wished him good luck.

On May 3, leaving his militia, the New Haven Guards, behind, Arnold rode west at the head of a pack train. A few other militiamen accompanied him.[4] They took less than three days to haul the supplies 110 miles from Cambridge to Williamstown on the Massachusetts-Vermont border. On the way, Arnold learned that his was not the only expedition against Fort Ticonderoga.

Ethan Allen and the Green Mountain Boys

Ethan Allen, a powerful six-footer from Vermont, was leading about one hundred thirty of his friends, the Green Mountain Boys, on the same mission. Ironically, this was due in part to Arnold's own actions. On the road to Boston from New Haven, Arnold had met Samuel Parsons, another patriot from Connecticut. They had discussed the colonists' desperate need for cannons. Arnold had mentioned the cannons at Fort Ticonderoga to Parsons, who then traveled on to Hartford, Connecticut. In Hartford, Parsons had convinced other patriots to join him in supporting an expedition against Fort Ticonderoga. Ethan Allen had been persuaded to lead the expedition.

News of Allen's expedition did not reach Arnold or the members of the Massachusetts Committee of Safety until after Arnold had left Boston. The news that Allen's expedition was ahead of him was especially terrible for Arnold because he saw *himself* as the leader of the glorious victory to come.[5]

Arnold left his militiamen and supplies at Williamstown. Alone, he rode fifteen miles through the spring mud and over the mountains to Castleton, Vermont. There, some of the Green Mountain Boys were organizing supplies and reinforcements for Ethan Allen and his men.

When he rode up to the tavern that the Green Mountain Boys were using as a headquarters, Arnold jumped off his exhausted horse and demanded to see the officer in charge. He explained that he had the authority of the Massachusetts Committee of Safety to lead the expedition against Fort Ticonderoga. He demanded that the Green Mountain Boys recognize his authority.

They told him that they recognized no commander but their own. They also asked him whether he actually had any troops to command. He replied that his captains were still in western Massachusetts, recruiting volunteers. He continued to stand his ground and demand respect as an officer. The Green Mountain Boys told him that Ethan Allen was at Shoreham, the starting place for the attack on Fort Ticonderoga. Arnold would have to settle the matter with Allen, not with them.[6]

Arnold caught up with Ethan Allen at Shoreham on May 9, 1775. Again Arnold demanded to lead the expedition. Eventually, Allen seems to have suggested that they share command. Allen's men, however, protested. Finally, Allen offered Arnold command of a column of his men as a volunteer officer. The matter was settled. Arnold was determined to participate, somehow, in the battle.

Allen's men spent May 9 searching for boats in the area. In the middle of the night, they began to make their move from the east bank of Lake Champlain to the west, where Fort Ticonderoga sat. At 3:00 A.M., Allen, Arnold, and forty men climbed into the lead boat. It was raining. Almost sinking under the weight, the boat sailed across the lake and unloaded passengers. The boat then returned to the other side, picked up another load of men, and took them across.

It was now almost 5:00 A.M. on May 10. The sky was beginning to lighten in the east. They could wait no longer. Leading just over eighty men, Arnold and Allen sneaked up under the fort's eastern wall. Then they ran for the front gate. Finding it locked, they opened the wicket next to it and hurried through the low tunnel that led under the fort's walls and into its interior.[7]

Storming Fort Ticonderoga

Just one British sentry saw the American soldiers coming. He shouted an alarm, but it was too late. The patriots rushed in. The men ran into the barracks.

With Ethan Allen and the Green Mountain Boys, Arnold captured Fort Ticonderoga in a battle that took only ten minutes. This is an artist's depiction of the fort's surrender to Allen.

Each British soldier suddenly woke to find a rifle pointed at his head.

Arnold and Allen rushed for the stairs that led to the officers' quarters.[8] There, they met half-dressed Lieutenant Jocelyn Feltham, who demanded to know by what authority they had entered the fort. "In the name of the great Jehovah and the Continental Congress," Ethan Allen later claimed he had bellowed.[9] The commander of the fort, Captain William Delaplace, finally appeared. He surrendered the fort, his sword, and his pistols.

The Battle of Ticonderoga was over. It had taken just ten minutes.[10] No one had been killed. The Americans had made a bold strike and had scored a significant, yet bloodless, victory against the British. And Benedict Arnold had played a role in the first American victory in the war.

2

THE EARLY YEARS

Benedict Arnold was born on January 14, 1741, in Norwich, Connecticut. He was the fifth member of his family to bear his name: his great-great-grandfather, great-grandfather, grandfather, and father all had the same name.

Born in Rhode Island, his father belonged to an important family. Benedict Arnold's great-great-grandfather had been one of Rhode Island's founders and owned a huge amount of land in the colony. His great-grandfather was elected governor of Rhode Island ten times, holding the office for a total of fifteen years. No other individual has ever held the office for that long.[1]

By the time Benedict's father had become an adult, however, the family owned much less property. The Arnold land holdings had been split among many descendants. Benedict's father's parents could not give him enough money to start a business of his own, so he became an apprentice. Apprenticeship was then the way many young men prepared for a career. During an apprenticeship, which generally lasted seven years, a young man worked for an experienced artisan, learning a skill. An apprentice received no pay for his labor, but he did get room and board. Arnold agreed to work seven years for a cooper (barrel maker).[2]

Around 1730, the elder Benedict Arnold left his apprenticeship unfinished. He boarded a sloop bound for Norwich, Connecticut, a new inland port on what was then the frontier. There, he set up a barrel shop on the Chelsea Wharf. Histories of Norwich say he soon expanded his business, entering a partnership with Captain Absalom King, who owned ships that sailed to islands in the Caribbean Sea and the British Isles, where King bought and sold a wide variety of goods.[3]

Benedict Arnold's Mother

In 1732, Absalom King disappeared at sea. A year later, in November 1733, Arnold married King's widow, Hannah. She was the daughter of one of Norwich's leading families. She already had a

Connecticut

The colony of Connecticut was founded when the frontier settlements of Hartford, Windsor, and Wethersfield banded together under a single government. Previously these towns had been part of Massachusetts. When Benedict Arnold's father arrived in Norwich, around 1730, Connecticut was more settled, but it remained part of the American frontier.

daughter, also named Hannah. The new couple soon had a son they named Benedict. However, the children both died, on the same day. Many epidemics swept New England during this period. The exact cause of the children's deaths, however, is no longer known.[4]

The Arnolds went on to have more children. In 1741, they had a second son, whom they also named Benedict. A year later, in December 1742, they had a daughter, another Hannah. Six more children followed, but only Benedict and Hannah would live to adulthood.

The Family Flourishes

When his children were little, Captain Benedict Arnold's business was flourishing. Thanks to his marriage, he now owned Absalom King's ships, shipyard, and warehouse. He was able to build a large house for his family—one with twelve rooms and eight fireplaces.

The Arnolds belonged to the Congregational Church in Norwich. When Benedict Arnold and Hannah King married, they were not full members of the church. During the Great Awakening, a period when great religious fervor swept the area, they sought full church membership. They attended services with their children several times a week. The Arnold family occupied a private pew, a sign that they were well respected in their community. Mrs. Arnold, in particular, was very pious. Even as an adult, her son Benedict kept letters she had written him as a child, warning him that he must always fight the temptation to sin. "[How] soon sickness and death may meet you, you nor I don't know," she wrote. "Prepare to meet your God before your feet stumble on ye dark mountains."[5]

Benedict Arnold had a bronze complexion, dark hair, and blue eyes.[6] His hawklike nose was the outstanding feature of his face. He stood five feet four or five feet five as an adult. In his day, he would have been average in height. As a child, Benedict Arnold was healthy and active. He and his friends played outside a great deal. They loved to go sledding. He skated for hours when the local rivers froze, building powerful leg muscles. In the summer, he fished, swam, and explored the wharves. He became used to the outdoors and vigorous exercise.[7]

School

Benedict Arnold's intelligence became evident early during his active childhood years. At first, his parents sent him to a teacher named Dr. Jewett, who taught his pupils elementary grammar and arithmetic and to write well. Norwich historian William Stanley says Arnold also attended Prudence Crandall's school in the nearby town of Canterbury.[8]

By this time, Captain Arnold, Benedict's father, had begun to suffer setbacks in his business. What colonists called King George's War had begun. European powers Great Britain and Holland fought against France and Spain over the question of who should take the throne in Austria. Eventually, the fighting reached the Western Hemisphere, interrupting colonial trade with the Caribbean. This almost certainly affected Captain Arnold and other merchants and traders. He may have had to call off many voyages he had scheduled to the West Indies.[9] In the 1740s, Arnold may have become overextended in his business—buying more than he could sell.

Despite her husband's financial troubles, Hannah Arnold managed to save enough money to send young Benedict to a private school in nearby Canterbury in 1752. Reverend James Cogswell ran the school in his home. Cogswell was a classical scholar who had just graduated from Yale College. He instructed Arnold and the six or seven other students in Latin, Greek, English, mathematics, and religion.

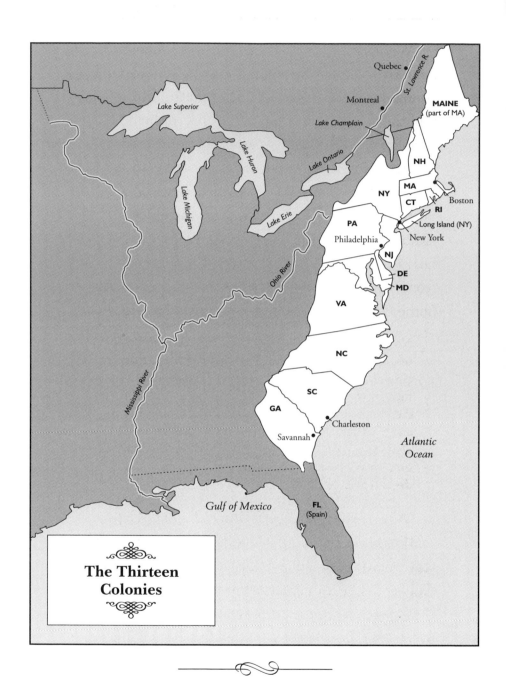

The Thirteen
Colonies

This map shows the thirteen British colonies in America as they looked during Benedict Arnold's youth.

While he was away at Cogswell's school in 1753, Arnold received extremely sad news. Two of his younger sisters, Mary and Elizabeth, had died of diphtheria. Around this time, his father, Captain Arnold, began to drink heavily. Some historians have speculated that the elder Arnold became an alcoholic because he was upset over his business setbacks. Historian William Wallace wrote, "the elder Benedict Arnold overextended his mercantile ventures, lost heavily, and consoled himself at the local taverns, from which his young son often had to lead him home."[10] Scholar James Kirby Martin has argued:

> No evidence exists to show that his drinking got out of control until after the diphtheria epidemic of 1753 claimed the lives of Mary and Elizabeth. A loving father, the Captain found the deaths of these two daughters and the lingering threat of losing Benedict and Hannah too difficult to bear. Great quantities of alcohol dulled his senses and temporarily eased the emotional pain associated with the ongoing devastation of his family.[11]

When they enrolled Benedict at Cogswell's school, his parents almost certainly expected him to stay there until he was old enough to go to Yale College. The boy stayed with Cogswell for only three years, however. At age fourteen, Benedict had to leave school. His mother and father had no more money for his education. He had begun to ride the roller coaster of success and failure that he would seemingly ride all his life.[12]

Apprentice Apothecary

By the time he returned to Norwich at age fourteen, Benedict had reached his full height. Having attained the size of a grown-up, he soon took on adult responsibilities as well. In 1756, his mother apprenticed her son to her cousins Daniel and Joshua Lathrop, who owned a very successful apothecary shop (drugstore). Arnold biographer Willard M. Wallace stated that Hannah Arnold made the apprentice arrangement because Benedict had become so rebellious she could no longer control him.[13] Perhaps, however, she simply realized that he would soon reach adulthood and would need to support himself. Since Hannah Arnold could no longer afford to send Benedict to school, she arranged for him to receive what amounted to job training.

Biographers have speculated that Benedict was mortified by his family's decline from riches to poverty. "[The] lad's private turmoil can be imagined," wrote historian Claire Brandt:

> Having confidently set forth from Norwich, the eldest son of a respectable family, to travel a path that he and everyone else fully expected to take him to the pinnacle of American society, he had been forced to return and face his friends and neighbors, the apprenticed son of a bankrupt and a drunk. His humiliation was severe; but like many adolescent agonies it remained buried, working its destruction secretly, silently and slowly, deep beneath the skin.[14]

Earlier, Benedict Arnold might have dreamed of becoming a scholar or perhaps a rich merchant like his father had been. But for the time being, he worked as an apothecary, growing herbs and making medicines and powders. Nevertheless, his quick mind and attention to detail made him an asset to the Lathrop firm.[15]

In 1757, the Lathrops gave Benedict permission to accompany soldiers from Norwich to Fort William Henry on Lake George, which had been attacked by the French-led Mohawk people as part of the French and Indian War. After marching for a week, however, the Norwich men arrived too late to see any action. Arnold and the other men from Norwich went home.

Eventually, the Lathrops assigned Arnold new duties. They used him to buy and sell cargo on several of their trading ventures to London and the Caribbean. He did business for the Lathrops in many different ports. These voyages helped him develop a love for the sea.

In 1759, Hannah Arnold, Benedict's mother, died. Then in 1761, his father, by then the town drunk, died. A year before his death, he had been arrested for public drunkenness. The Congregational Church had also admonished him for his drinking.[16]

In January 1762, the younger Benedict Arnold came of age and was released from servitude to the Lathrops. He had inherited almost nothing from his parents. After his father's death, the Arnolds' house had been sold to pay debts. When Benedict's apprenticeship came to an end, the Lathrops loaned him money to start his own business. They gave him £500 in credit, then a small fortune, with which to buy supplies. He sailed to London to purchase what he would need.[17]

Arnold in the French and Indian War

Many biographies say that as a young man, Benedict Arnold ran away from the Lathrops to fight in what the American colonists called the French and Indian War.[18] One morning, he seems to have set off on foot for Westchester, New York, having told no one he was going to leave. His mother, having learned of his actions, had him forcibly brought home. The next year, supposedly, he again ran off to the army, only to have the Lathrops advertise a reward for his return.

Biographer James Kirby Martin, however, has denied such stories. He acknowledged that a Benedict Arnold from Norwalk, Connecticut, joined the Westchester militia. He believes this was a distant relative of Benedict Arnold of Norwich. Had Benedict Arnold wanted to join, he points out, there were many militias seeking members closer to his hometown. Martin also doubts that Arnold ever ran away from the Lathrops. They always spoke very highly of him.[19]

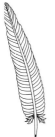

On His Own

Upon returning from Europe in 1762, Benedict Arnold moved to New Haven, where he opened his own apothecary shop. There, he could enjoy his new independence. Home to Yale College, New Haven was then the fastest-growing town in Connecticut. The sign Arnold hung above his door declared him a druggist. In fact, the people of New Haven found his medical advice so satisfactory that many called him "Doctor" Arnold.[20] He stocked not just herbs and medicines but cosmetics, jewelry, and stationery. He also sold books, many of which he read himself, to Yale students and professors.

In the fall of 1763, Arnold returned to Norwich on a visit and bought back his family estate. It clearly held no great sentimental value for him, however. In March 1764, he sold the property, making a tidy profit.[21] He reimbursed the Lathrops for the loan they had made him when he went into business. Around this time, he arranged for his sister, Hannah, to move to New Haven. They would share a close relationship throughout their lives.

Hannah was bright and hardworking. Because she could run his house and business when he was away, Arnold and a silent partner named Adam Babcock bought a forty-ton brigantine named *Fortune*. The French and Indian War had ended with a British victory, and Americans—British subjects—were once again profiting from trading in the West Indies and elsewhere. Craving money and adventure, Arnold wanted to expand his business. He and his crew of sailors made many voyages to the Caribbean and to Canada, where Arnold sold livestock and lumber and bought commodities such as salt and cotton, which he could sell easily back in the American colonies. Sometimes during his early years in business, Arnold lacked "hard money."[22] Nevertheless, by 1765, Arnold and Babcock also owned the thirty-ton *Charming Sally* and the twenty-eight-ton *Three Brothers*. By the early 1770s, business was booming.

Once, Arnold got into terrible trouble in Honduras. In port, he was invited to a party by an important British sea captain named Croskie. Arnold did not attend, because he had to get papers in order so that he could set sail the next day. The next morning, however, he rowed to Croskie's ship to apologize for his failure to come to the party. His arrival angered Croskie. In front of a crowd, Croskie called Arnold "a damned Yankee" and demanded to know why he had no manners.[23]

Arnold took this as a serious offense to his personal honor, and immediately challenged Croskie to a duel. At sunrise the next morning, Arnold, his seconds, and a surgeon waited for Croskie and his seconds on an island in the Bay of Honduras. Finally, they saw Croskie approaching in a boat. Arnold, infuriated by the fact that Croskie had brought several big, burly men with him, cocked his pistols and threatened to shoot Croskie's companions if they came any closer. Croskie waved them off and came ashore with just his official seconds. As the challenged party, Croskie took the first shot and missed. Arnold's first shot grazed Croskie's arm. Before they could take a second shot, Croskie apologized for insulting his opponent. Arnold accepted. This incident well illustrates the extent to which Arnold valued his honor.

In addition to his personal problems, Arnold had a lot of trouble with the British. After the end of the French and Indian War, Great Britain began to make outrageous demands on the American colonies, curtailing colonial trade and taxing the colonists' goods. This so angered many colonial traders that they began to operate outside of the law, ignoring British trade restrictions. Like many others, Arnold, resenting Great Britain's actions, became a smuggler.[24]

3

ARNOLD BECOMES A REBEL

In the mid-1760s, virtually every ship owner living in the American colonies dealt in contraband, or illegal, goods. In 1764, the British government had passed the Sugar Act, requiring all ship captains to send raw goods from the colonies to England before sending them to other places in Europe. This severely limited the profits Americans could make exporting goods. In 1765, Great Britain passed the Stamp Act. It required shippers to pay customs officials for special stamps that had to be put on almost all types of official papers and even items such as newspapers.

Historians believe Arnold broke the law and smuggled goods in order to avoid paying trade duties.

In this he was hardly alone. He and most other New England merchants felt breaking the law was justified not only because they needed to make a living, but because they felt the laws were unfairly placed upon the American colonists.

Accused!

In 1766, Benedict Arnold's ship was almost confiscated by British customs officials. One of his sailors, Peter Boles, threatened to tell the authorities that he knew sailors working for Arnold who had sneaked goods—probably barrels of molasses—onshore. If Arnold bribed him, Boles said, he would keep silent about what he saw on board Arnold's ship, the *Fortune*. Otherwise, he would turn in Arnold to the authorities.[1] Arnold refused to pay the blackmail. As a result, on Saturday, January 24, 1766, Boles went to the customs house in New Haven, the port where Arnold's business was based. Boles intended to tell customs commissioner David Wooster that the *Fortune* carried illegal cargo. He expected that British officials would then seize the ship and sell it, along with its cargo. As an informer, he hoped to receive a portion of these profits.

However, Boles's plan did not work. Wooster was not in his office. Boles realized he would have to wait to turn in Arnold. But by Monday morning, Arnold had learned what Boles intended to do. Other sailors from the *Fortune* helped Arnold find

Boles. They did not want to be turned in, either. Dragging Boles outside, in Arnold's words, they "gave him a little chastisement [punishment]."[2] They probably expected that the beating would convince Boles to leave town. But he stayed.

That night, a group of merchants found Boles and forced him to sign a statement Arnold had written. In signing it, Boles said he had been "instigated by the Devil" (inspired by Satan) and promised never again to turn in anyone for smuggling.[3] He also swore he would leave New Haven immediately. However, he did not do so. Arnold found out around midnight that Boles was still in town. An angry party, including Arnold and members of his ship's crew, caught Boles once again. This time, they tied him to a post and whipped him forty times.[4]

Learning of this whipping, town elders ordered a grand jury to decide whether Arnold and his companions should be arrested. The grand jury indicted the men. Townspeople protested, carrying torches and shouting, to show support for Arnold and his men. Nevertheless, the town court found Arnold guilty. However, the justice of the peace fined Arnold only fifty shillings—a small amount of money—for disturbing the peace.[5] Later that night, there was another demonstration supporting Arnold. He had become a hero to many of the people of New Haven.

Arnold's Politics

Arnold was growing angry at the way the British government treated the American colonies. Arnold considered the British laws applying to trade particularly unfair. After the British passed the Stamp Act, Arnold submitted articles to the Connecticut *Gazette*. He argued that the Magna Carta—a document guaranteeing certain liberties granted by King John of England in 1215, which is still recognized in Great Britain today—guaranteed all Englishmen (including colonists) rights that the Sugar Act and Stamp Act violated. At the same time, Arnold began to correspond with other patriots, discussing important political matters.

Arnold Starts a Family

By March 1766, Arnold had become engaged to Margaret "Peggy" Mansfield. She was the daughter of a prosperous trader named Samuel Mansfield. Mansfield also served as the town's high sheriff.[6] Marriage to Peggy Mansfield meant that Arnold would take a step up in society.

The couple married in 1767. Hannah Arnold lived with them. On February 14, 1768, Peggy Arnold gave birth to a son they named Benedict. Within a year, she became pregnant again. Their second son, Richard, was born in August 1769. The Arnolds had a third son, Henry, in 1772.[7]

The British passed the Stamp Act in 1765, which affected trade and became the cause of violent protest. This cartoon depicts the American response to British taxes on trade goods.

Throughout their marriage, Benedict and Peggy Arnold had financial troubles. In 1766, it looked like American merchants could expect to make more money after the Stamp Act was repealed. But in 1767, new British customs regulations called the Townshend Acts severely limited the kinds of goods colonial ship owners could trade. By the end of the year, Arnold's business was in such bad shape that he was close to fifteen hundred pounds in debt.[8]

After 1770, things began to look up for merchants again. Arnold borrowed heavily to build his family a new house on Water Street, one of New Haven's most fashionable streets. But even as contractors worked on the house's fancy high ceilings and curved staircase, the British announced new taxes. The new Tea Act halted trade. Arnold had to stop work on the new house.

At the same time, Arnold's father-in-law faced financial ruin. Hearing news of Samuel Mansfield's bankruptcy while away on business, Arnold wrote to his wife to forbid her to loan her father any money and to beg her to keep their children in school. He still remembered very clearly the humiliation of having to leave school when his father went bankrupt.[9]

Militiaman

As the 1770s began, Arnold remained committed to the cause of liberty for the colonists. On June 9,

1770, he wrote, "Good God, are the Americans all asleep & tamely giving up their glorious liberties or, are they all turned Philosophers that they don't take immediate vengeance on such miscreants; I am afraid of the latter. . . ."[10] He wanted the colonists to take revenge on the British for imposing the unfair taxes and hurting colonial business.

In December 1773, the Boston Tea Party, in which colonists dumped tea into Boston Harbor to protest a tax on the drink, started a chain reaction that would end in revolution. In 1774, delegates gathered for the First Continental Congress.

Throughout these years, Arnold was always a patriot, supporting the colonists in the fight against Great Britain. Just after New Year's Day in 1775, anticipating war, approximately sixty citizens of New Haven formed a local militia called the Governor's Fort Guards.[11] Arnold not only helped organize the militia, but was elected its captain.

Arnold took his command seriously. An intelligent, scholarly man, he read many accounts of former wars. Like George Washington, who would be appointed Commander in Chief of the American forces, he studied the exploits of great generals like Julius Caesar, Alexander the Great, and Hannibal.[12] At the same time, he drilled his men, marching them around the New Haven green, or town square.

The American Revolution began on April 19, 1775, when British soldiers, under orders to seize colonists' military supplies, fought colonial militiamen first in Lexington and then in Concord, Massachusetts. Even as the fighting in Lexington and Concord was taking place, riders raced to spread the news of the British attack to the rest of the American colonies. The news reached New Haven, Connecticut, on April 21. Its townspeople gathered that night for an emergency town meeting. By vote, they decided the time had not yet come to send the town militia to Boston in support of the patriots. They wanted to know more about what had occurred at Lexington and Concord. However, the members of the militia, known officially as the Governor's Fort Guards, disagreed. At their own meeting on April 21, the members of the Guard voted to set off the next morning to join other colonists preparing to fight in Boston.[13]

Early on the morning of April 22, the Fort Guards gathered at the town square in front of a crowd of hundreds of townspeople. After a prayer led by a local minister, Benedict Arnold led his men to a tavern, where the town elders were meeting. Before they left, they wanted to open the local powder magazine to get arms and ammunition. Arnold sent a lieutenant inside to announce that the Guard was ready to depart for Boston. The elders, in turn, sent David Wooster, a member of the town council, to remind Arnold that the town had voted the night before to remain neutral, at least for the time

Paul Revere, seen here on his famous ride to warn American colonists that the British were coming, was another patriot who later got into trouble with the military. The charges against Revere—disobeying orders and "unsoldierlike" behavior—were later dismissed.

Lexington and Concord

The Battles of Lexington and Concord, both of which took place on April 19, 1775, were the result of British General Thomas Gage's order sending soldiers to seize ammunition colonists had stockpiled in Concord. In Lexington, colonial soldiers attempted to stop the British march. Seventy Americans faced seven hundred British soldiers. Eight colonists died. One British soldier was wounded. Later the same day, the British confronted more Americans in Concord. Serious fighting ensued. Colonists chased the British all the way back to Boston. In Concord and en route, 273 British soldiers died.

being. The Guard, therefore, could not have access to the arsenal. Arnold demanded its keys. "None but Almighty God shall prevent my marching!" he is said to have shouted at Wooster.[14]

The town elders gave in. Arnold and his men left New Haven with guns, powder, and flints.

Trouble for a Hero

After a long march, Arnold and his men, along with Ethan Allen and the Green Mountain Boys, succeeded in taking control of Fort Ticonderoga. Two days after the capture of Ticonderoga, on May 12, the Green Mountain Boys also captured nearby Crown Point, which had been, until 1773, the site of another British fort. It had been destroyed by

The Battles of Lexington (seen here) and Concord marked the beginning of the American Revolution.

fire, but some artillery remained there. Thanks to the action at Ticonderoga and Crown Point, the Americans gained 201 pieces of artillery, including 78 working cannons, 6 mortars, 3 howitzers, thousands of cannon balls, and 30,000 flints.[15] Eventually, fifty-seven of the cannons were hauled back to Boston.[16]

The victories of Arnold and Allen "created a sensation that gave the rebellion tremendous confidence and heart," wrote historian Benson Bobrick.[17] However, Arnold did not have an easy time after the expedition. His command was challenged.

On June 22, 1775, three delegates from Massachusetts arrived at Crown Point to investigate whether the forts in the area were important enough to "the general defense of these colonies" for the colony of Massachusetts to continue paying the expenses of Arnold and his regiment.[18] The delegates announced that Arnold should step down from his post so that Benjamin Hinman—who was from Massachusetts, whereas Arnold was from Connecticut—could take command. Should Arnold wish to remain there, they said, he would be second in command.[19] On June 24, 1775, Arnold disbanded his regiment. The men had not yet been fully paid. Arnold had spent £1,000 of his own to pay part of what they were owed. Many of his men stayed in Canada, not wanting to leave without their full pay. Arnold, however, returned to the colonies.

Back in the Colonies

On June 27, Congress voted to create a Northern Department of War. Its purpose was to form an army especially to fight on the Canadian-American border. Commander in Chief George Washington was concerned that, if the British moved troops from Boston to New York, they might make contact with the British soldiers stationed in Canada.[20] A British invasion from Canada might then occur. Major General Philip Schuyler was awarded the Northern Department's command.

General Philip Schuyler respected Arnold's military successes.

After returning from Canada, Arnold stopped in Albany, New York, to rest. There, he met Schuyler, who thought very highly of Arnold because of his achievements in the Lake Champlain region.[21] In July 1775, the two men discussed plans for an American invasion of Canada. Schuyler expressed his interest in helping Arnold obtain a new post in the army. Schuyler asked Arnold to serve as an adjutant general in his department. Interested in receiving this appointment, Arnold stayed in Albany. However, he received news that his wife, Peggy, had died.[22] Her father had died three days later. Now Arnold headed for New Haven. He wanted to return home to settle his personal affairs and check on his children—Benedict, seven; Richard, five; and Henry, three—who were being cared for by Arnold's sister, Hannah.

In New Haven, Benedict Arnold comforted his family. Together, they visited the graves of Peggy Arnold and Samuel Mansfield. Benedict and Hannah

Arnold also spent time reviewing his business affairs. Arnold had a sudden, terrible attack of gout, which left him unable to walk. For several days, he took to his bed. For a time, he considered leaving the military but finally decided "an idle life" would lead him to "a lingering death."[23] Arnold stayed home for less than three weeks.

On July 26, 1775, Benedict Arnold left New Haven for Massachusetts. On August 1, he appeared in Watertown before the Massachusetts Provincial Congress. He wanted the Congress to pay his salary for the months he had spent fighting around Lake Champlain, as well as reimbursement for expenses he had incurred there. For weeks, he haggled with a committee over how much was owed him. On August 19, the committee finally offered him a partial payment— he received just a fraction of what he had requested. (He would eventually receive the rest of his payment in January 1776 from the Continental Congress, not the Massachusetts legislative body.)

In mid-August, Arnold rode to nearby Cambridge, Massachusetts. There, Arnold met Commander in Chief George Washington at his headquarters. Washington had already heard of Arnold's performance at Ticonderoga. He found that he admired Arnold in person, too. They were both daring men who shared a great interest in warfare.

Together, they discussed the proposed invasion of Canada by American soldiers. Washington wanted to know everything Arnold knew about conditions in southern Quebec. Arnold also informed Washington of the military stores he and Allen had secured at Ticonderoga and Crown Point.[24]

Washington decided that Benedict Arnold should play an important role in the American invasion of Canada. Schuyler was planning a main attack from the Champlain forts. Washington wanted Arnold to lead a second force, which would come from the direction of Maine. As Washington biographer Douglas Southall Freeman wrote, upon meeting Arnold,

> Washington quickly saw that Arnold was furnished with much of the stuff that must be in a man called to head a swiftly-moving expedition that was to fight water and wind and winter. Besides as a trader before the war, Arnold had been to Quebec and probably knew more about the town and the approaches to it than did any officer of Washington's immediate command. Arnold could get there![25]

Letters flew between George Washington and Philip Schuyler concerning the final plans for the invasion of Canada. On August 20, 1775, Washington wrote to Schuyler about creating a diversion, but did not mention specifically that he wanted Arnold to lead the surprise second attack. Schuyler agreed to the plan.[26] In the meantime, Washington had told Arnold that he wanted him to lead the second force.[27]

Now all Arnold needed was a new place in the army. Washington nominated him for a colonelcy in

Continental Army Commander in Chief George Washington (seen here) admired Benedict Arnold for his leadership during the war.

the Continental Army, as the American army was called. When he did so, he made it clear to Arnold that he was to regard Schuyler as his superior officer and accept his authority.[28] Arnold agreed. The Continental Congress, in its turn, made his appointment. Arnold now held a position in the Continental Army.

QUEBEC AND SARATOGA

From late 1775 through the fall of 1777, Benedict Arnold paid little attention to his family. He was too busy leading the life of a soldier. His unmarried sister, Hannah, continued to care for his children at their home in New Haven. She also tended to his business affairs, keeping his books and making arrangements for his ships to deliver and pick up goods. She and Arnold wrote to each other frequently. He asked about the children and sent messages to his sons, whom he referred to as "dear innocent prattlers."[1] Hannah, in turn, told him of the many kisses they sent him and how proud they all were of his achievements.

The Campaign

In the meantime, Arnold, along with General Philip Schuyler and Commander in Chief George Washington, prepared for the American invasion of Canada. To get Arnold and his men ready to march before winter required a flurry of activity. Washington decided that Arnold should lead a force of about eleven hundred soldiers, including three companies of riflemen. When Washington announced to soldiers camped in Cambridge that he needed experienced woodsmen to accompany Arnold on his venture, hundreds volunteered. General Horatio Gates authorized the purchases of flour and meat that Arnold's troops needed. He also ordered flatboats built to carry Arnold's men up the Kennebec River.

All involved worked so hard and so fast that Arnold's troops were ready to march out of Cambridge through Medford, Salem, Danvers, and Ipswich, to Newburyport, starting on September 11.[2] Arnold himself received his final marching orders on September 14, 1775. By September 19, he was in Newburyport, watching his men board eleven boats. There was not enough wind that day to set sail, but twenty-four hours later, all the boats set off.

This stage in their journey proved "very troublesome."[3] Rainstorms made the seas rough. Many of his soldiers had never been aboard a ship and suffered terribly from seasickness. Once they entered the Kennebec River, some vessels got separated from the group and, entering the wrong river channel, got stuck in mud. By nightfall on September 22, however, all were docked in Gardinerstown.

Here, they found the two hundred bateaux Gates had had constructed for them. The entire column loaded their supplies into these small, flat-bottomed boats and set off once more. Over the next three weeks, they traveled upriver, paddling the boats whenever possible. In some places, however, river rapids made passage by water too dangerous, and the soldiers had to portage, carrying their boats over muddy ground. The boats, which had been built quickly from green wood, soon started to leak. The men got wet and their rations

Arnold led a force of eleven hundred men, planning to invade Quebec from Maine. The trip, depicted here, was a strenuous one.

soaked. At night, the temperature often fell below freezing. By the time they reached Norridgewock Falls, a hundred men were sick with colds, fevers, and dysentery.[4] Beyond lay no settlements, only wilderness.

Arnold worked hard to keep up morale and pushed his troops on beyond what was called the Great Carrying Place, a final, exhausting portage. On October 19, heavy rains started to fall, causing the river to rise three feet. Within the next two days, it rose another eight feet. On October 23, the weather had cleared but Arnold's men had lost most of their remaining supplies. Many were sick. Nevertheless, when Arnold gathered his officers together for a council of war, they voted to continue on toward Quebec.[5] By October 25, they were in the mountains. Now they had to march over stones and rocks covered with ice and snow, still carrying bateaux. Once over the heights, they put their boats back into the water. Finally, on October 31, 1775, they reached Canada's Chaudiere River, where they met some French inhabitants of Canada.[6]

On November 15, Arnold and his men arrived outside Quebec. En route, hundreds had become sick from drinking contaminated water. They had faced such hunger that the men had eaten candles, shoe leather, and even a dog. In the face of such adversity, at least three hundred men had turned back. Others died along the way. By the time he reached Quebec, Arnold was left with only about six hundred fifty men in his command.[7]

Nonetheless, Arnold had proven himself to be a courageous leader. But he could not immediately attack the city of Quebec. He lacked artillery and manpower.

Quebec

In the fall at Ticonderoga, Major General Philip Schuyler and Brigadier General Richard Montgomery had assembled the men they would lead to attack Montreal and Quebec. Montgomery and Schuyler encountered many difficulties that winter. Montgomery grew tired of waiting while Schuyler prepared to leave Fort Ticonderoga, so he set out without the general. Twelve hundred men accompanied him.

Schuyler soon entered Canada, too, with about eight hundred troops. Schuyler became terribly ill, however, and was forced to retreat back across the Canadian border.

Montgomery took charge of all their troops. For forty-five miserable days, Montgomery and his men laid siege to Fort St. Jean. Heavy rain led Montgomery to write, "We have been like half-drowned rats crawling through a swamp."[8] Eventually, the British soldiers stationed at the fort surrendered. They were starving. Montgomery then marched his men to Montreal. The British commander at Montreal, Guy Carleton, fled to Quebec.

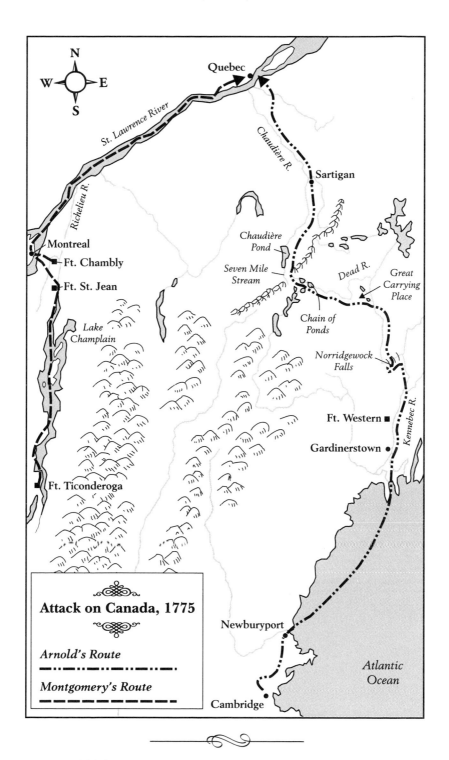

Arnold led troops into Canada by way of Maine, which proved to be an unsuccessful and costly battle.

Siege

On December 2, Montgomery's forces finally met Arnold's troops. The combined forces then laid siege to Quebec. Unfortunately for the Americans, the British were well-equipped inside the walled city. They had reinforced its fortifications and positioned a hundred cannons to fire at their attackers. For a time, the Americans fought from within a fort they had built of ice.[9] It collapsed under artillery fire, however, on December 15. The Americans suffered from exposure, lice, and smallpox. Blizzards made conditions especially miserable.

On December 30, Montgomery commanded the American troops in an outright assault on Quebec. His attack proved poorly planned. He and Arnold each led half of the army into town, from opposite directions. Unfortunately, the enemy discovered their plans beforehand. The Americans suffered a terrible defeat. Cannons killed many Americans even before they entered the city's gates. Others died in hand-to-hand combat inside. The British captured 426 American soldiers. Another sixty died that day. Montgomery was among the dead. Arnold suffered a terrible injury when a musket ball shattered the bones in his lower left leg.

American soldiers deserted in droves. But some regrouped outside of Quebec. After recuperating for a short time in a field hospital, Arnold assumed command of the remaining troops. He and his troops

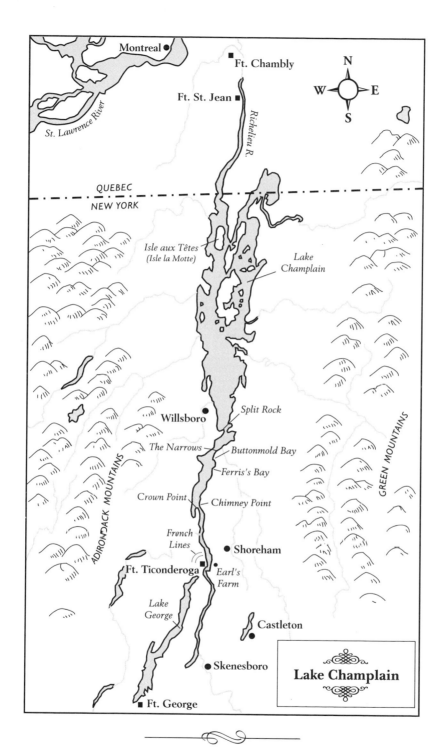

Montreal

Ft. Chambly

Ft. St. Jean

Richelieu R.

St. Lawrence River

N
W E
S

QUEBEC
NEW YORK

Isle aux Têtes
(Isle la Motte)

Lake
Champlain

ADIRONDACK MOUNTAINS

GREEN MOUNTAINS

Willsboro

Split Rock

The Narrows

Buttonmold Bay

Ferris's Bay

Crown Point

Chimney Point

French
Lines

Shoreham

Ft. Ticonderoga

Earl's
Farm

Lake
George

Castleton

Skenesboro

Ft. George

Lake Champlain

In the campaign to gain control of Quebec, Brigadier General Richard Montgomery led a forty-five-day siege at Fort St. Jean at the north end of Lake Champlain before the British surrendered.

laid siege to Quebec for the rest of the winter. They made the lives of its residents miserable, cutting off supplies and communication with the rest of the world. In recognition of Arnold's military valor and ability, the Continental Congress promoted Arnold to brigadier general. Soon, however, he asked his superiors for help. He wanted reinforcements and someone else to assume command. He admitted that he did not know what to do next.

On April 1, 1776, General David Wooster arrived to take over. Arnold rode to Montreal. There, he met Benjamin Franklin, who, without success, was trying to persuade the Canadians, also British colonists, to support the American colonies in the fight against Great Britain.

On May 10, the British landed new troops. As British General John Burgoyne and four thousand fresh troops neared Quebec, the American soldiers under Wooster retreated toward the border. Legend has it that on June 18, 1776, Arnold became the very last American to leave Canada, waiting until he could hear thundering hooves and see the red coats of the British soldiers before retreating.[10]

Independence

Even after the Battles of Lexington and Concord, many Americans had remained hopeful that the colonies would reconcile with Great Britain. Gradually, however, a move for independence had gained support. On July 2, 1776, the Second Continental Congress voted to create the United States of America, declaring the former colonies a new nation, independent of British rule. Two days later, its members signed the Declaration of Independence, drafted by Thomas Jefferson, the statement explaining the Americans' reasons for separation.

Benedict Arnold spent the summer of 1776 following orders from General Washington to construct a fleet at Skenesboro (today Whitehall), New York.[11] This became America's first fleet of military ships. After the American evacuation of Canada, Arnold had gone to see Philip Schuyler, commander of the army's Northern Department. Washington, Schuyler, and Arnold all believed British troops would soon march south from Canada into the colonies. They hoped word of Arnold's fleet would cause the British to pause.[12]

Battle of Valcour Island

By mid-September, Benedict Arnold had several ships on Lake Champlain, practicing maneuvers. On October 11, British General Guy Carleton put his own ships into the water. Suddenly, they encountered the American fleet in Valcour Bay and a battle ensued. The Americans suffered badly, with sixty dead and many wounded.

Toward evening, the American officers met on Arnold's flagship. They knew their ammunition was about to run out. Some wanted to surrender. Others preferred to fight to the death.

Arnold, however, came up with a daring plan of escape. Under cover of darkness, his ships began to slip away toward Schuyler's Island. In the morning, Carleton discovered their absence and pursued them. New battles broke out.

Lagging behind the others, Arnold's ship and four smaller boats came under fire. Arnold refused to surrender, however. Instead, he ordered the vessels beached and burned. Their crews escaped overland to Fort Ticonderoga.

The British claimed victory in the Battle of Valcour. Yet Arnold made an important achievement

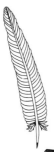

An Archaeological Discovery

In 1997, underwater archaeologists discovered the last remaining American warship from Benedict Arnold's 1776 Battle of Valcour Island. Arnold commanded a fleet of fifteen American warships during that battle. Some were destroyed in the fighting; Arnold himself ordered others destroyed when it became clear that defeat was at hand. Only four American vessels survived. This gunboat rests intact on the bottom of Lake Champlain. Underwater photography and videotapes reveal that the gunboat is in an excellent state of preservation, with its bow gun in place and its mast still standing over fifty feet above the lake bottom.

there. Thanks to Arnold's ability and perseverance, Carleton decided to delay his campaign against the American colonies. He thought Arnold might next use his men to cut British supply lines or build a new fleet. Arnold had, in essence, bought his new country time it desperately needed to prepare for a British assault. His actions helped allow the United States to stay in the war.

Saratoga

In 1777, Benedict Arnold returned to Canada as part of a new campaign. He was attached to the command of Major General Horatio Gates. In September, word reached Gates's headquarters on Bemis Heights that the British Army was on the move under the command of General John Burgoyne. In what became known as the Battle of Saratoga, on September 19, British and American soldiers suddenly met on a farm owned by a man named John Freeman.

After the initial battle began, Gates and Arnold had an argument when Gates did not acknowledge Arnold's contribution in the battle. Arnold was told to stay in his tent, after asking permission to leave.[13] A messenger arrived with word that the battle was in stalemate—neither side seemed to be winning, Arnold jumped on his horse and rode for the battle-field. Fighting ceased only at nightfall. Ultimately, no one had won. But later, British officers recorded that

General Horatio Gates was given most of the credit for victory at the Battle of Saratoga, despite the fact that Arnold strongly encouraged American soldiers to continue the fight.

they were impressed by the Americans' courage. They knew now that they could not expect the Americans to run from a fight.

After Arnold returned from that first day of fighting, Gates punished Arnold for disobeying his orders. Arnold was relieved of his command. Nevertheless, Arnold refused to return to the United States. Directly defying Gates's orders, he took part in the second day of the Battle of Saratoga. When the British and Americans met again on the battlefield on October 7, Arnold inspired American soldiers to fight wildly. He rode among them on a huge white horse, shouting encouragement and leading charges. Finally, the Americans defeated the British forces. In the heat of battle, Arnold suffered another wound in his left leg.

In the aftermath of Saratoga, Burgoyne surrendered 5,752 British soldiers, 42 cannons, and 7,000

A wounded Benedict Arnold is seen here at center, in action at the Battle of Saratoga.

muskets to the Americans.[14] The Battle of Saratoga was a stunning victory for the Americans. Although Gates received most of the credit for the American success, British General Burgoyne himself stated that it was mainly Arnold's victory. Asked about his decision to surrender, Burgoyne simply said, referring to Arnold, "It was his doing."[15]

Bitterness

Despite his heroic actions in Canada, Benedict Arnold made many enemies while in Canada. When he returned to the United States, he faced a court-martial on charges that he had mismanaged army funds. George Washington commended Arnold for his part in the Battle of Saratoga. But Arnold had to fight for months to regain his command. In the meantime, he brooded over what he saw as his mistreatment. He became a bitter man.[16]

5

PHILADELPHIA AND PEGGY SHIPPEN

On May 11, 1778, despite the continuing pain he suffered from his leg wound, Benedict Arnold returned to active duty in the Continental Army. On May 21, he arrived at General Washington's headquarters at Valley Forge, Pennsylvania. The men welcomed him as a hero.

George Washington immediately asked him to accept a new assignment. Washington knew that Arnold, who still could not stand on his own, was unable to fight actively.[1] Washington suggested instead that Arnold become the military governor of Philadelphia, then the United States capital. For most of the years of the American Revolution so far,

Philadelphia had been occupied by the British Army. But in the spring of 1778, the Redcoats, as the British soldiers were called, were preparing to evacuate the city and establish new headquarters in New York.[2]

Benedict Arnold Goes to Philadelphia

Arnold eagerly accepted the post. He took the oath of office on May 30 and arrived in Philadelphia on June 19.[3] The last British soldiers had left the city just one day earlier.

A short while later, Arnold's sister, Hannah, and his youngest son, Henry, now seven, came to live with him. His two older boys were then away at boarding school. Once again, Hannah would keep house for Arnold, act as his hostess when he entertained, and aid him with his business.

Governor

Arnold found the city of Philadelphia in sorry shape. The British had burned most of the wood available—cutting down trees, toppling fences, and even taking the pews from churches. Squares and commons were covered with mud. There was a huge mass grave near Independence Hall, where the British had buried two thousand American prisoners of war who had died in their custody.

Arnold moved into the mansion built by the Penn family, who had founded Pennsylvania, which a British general had just vacated. His new position required him to govern the city, to try to keep peace, and to manage supplies for the American soldiers posted there. Unfortunately, Arnold did not make a good governor. He had trouble keeping his own finances and those of the state separate.

While acting as governor, Arnold pursued his own business interests. He speculated in real estate, buying property he hoped to resell at a profit.[4] A merchant named Robert Shewell applied to Arnold for a pass to permit his ship, the *Charming Nancy*, to sail out of Philadelphia loaded with sugar, salt, tea, and glass—goods very much in demand. Arnold not only granted Shewell the pass but also bought a large share of his cargo. He later profited enormously from its sale.[5] He went into business with the army's "clothier general," buying goods the army did not need at a low price and reselling them to the public for much more.[6]

Romance

Like the British officers who had been there just weeks earlier, Arnold enjoyed making the rounds of Philadelphia society while he was governor. With Hannah acting as his hostess, he threw parties at his house. He enjoyed going to others' parties and dances, too, where young women flocked to his side. He was, after all, an eligible bachelor, a war hero, and a powerful man in the city.

Soon Arnold met Margaret Shippen. Margaret "Peggy" Shippen was born on June 11, 1760. She had one brother and five sisters. Her family was rich and illustrious. Her mother, also named Peggy, was gracious and well mannered. Her father, Edward, was a judge. He was descended from a prominent family of people who had been living in the colony since 1668. By the time the American Revolution broke out, he was chief justice of Pennsylvania. A scholarly man, he was a worrier by nature. This led him to be politically conservative. He took no public stand either for or against the British.

Peggy and her siblings were raised in the lap of luxury, even though they lived during a time of political turmoil. They lived in a richly furnished mansion maintained by servants. At times during the American Revolution, the Shippen family abandoned their home in Philadelphia. They were suspected of Toryism (remaining loyal to Great Britain). Edward

Tories

How many loyalists lived in the United States during the American Revolution? Historians estimate that, when the Declaration of Independence was signed, 20 percent of the colonial population either actively resisted the rebellion as Tories or supported it only when threatened with fines or imprisonment if they did not.

Shippen feared capture or destruction of his property. When the British took Philadelphia, the Shippen family moved back to their home.

By this time, Peggy was old enough to move about in society. She attended events where she met many British officers, some of whom her father invited to dine with the family. Peggy was a very intelligent woman with style and wit, and she liked to dress up and flirt. Often she annoyed her father by wanting to spend a lot of money on clothing. A tiny blonde, she was often described not just as a beauty, but as fascinatingly dainty. Many gentlemen declared their love for her.

Rumors began to fly of a romance between Peggy Shippen and Benedict Arnold. These rumors proved true. Arnold invited Peggy for many carriage rides and visited her at home. In March 1779, Peggy agreed to marry him. He then purchased an estate nearby, intending to make it their future

Peggy Shippen Arnold, Benedict Arnold's second wife.

residence. They would need a big house—Hannah and Henry Arnold would live with them. Sometimes the older Arnold boys would also come to visit.

Marriage

On April 8, 1779, Benedict Arnold and Peggy Shippen were married at Edward Shippen's home. She was eighteen years old. He was thirty-eight. Soon after their marriage, Arnold would take the first step toward taking part in one of the most notorious conspiracies in American history.

6

CHANGING SIDES

During his term as military governor and his courtship of Peggy Shippen, Benedict Arnold made many enemies. Many American patriots strongly protested the tolerance he showed many Tories. However, in June 1778, George Washington had written to Arnold instructing him that, in his role as governor,

> You will take every prudent step in your power to preserve tranquillity and order in the city and give security to individuals of every class and description; restraining, as far as possible, till the restoration of civil government, every species of persecution, insult or abuse, either from the soldiery to the inhabitants or among each other.[1]

Enemies

In 1778, matters began to come to a head. In August, Pennsylvania's representatives in the Continental Congress complained about Arnold's signing passes that allowed Tories to leave the state. Congress sided with the delegation and, on August 18, ordered Arnold to issue no more passes unless they were also signed by a state authority. Arnold was offended. He saw this as both a challenge to military authority and a personal insult.

A campaign against Arnold was then launched in print. Beginning in November, the *Pennsylvania Packet* newspaper ran a series of articles criticizing Arnold. The first denounced him for inviting the wives of Tories to his parties. A second article revealed that Arnold had been profiting from prize ships.

On December 1, Joseph Reed, a member of Congress who had long complained about Arnold, took office as president of Pennsylvania. He was one of a growing number of patriots who not only fought the British but protested the British way of life as it was practiced by colonial merchants and artisans. As president, Reed continued to attack Arnold. He wrote to General Washington, complaining that Arnold, seeking to profit, had made a deal with four sailors who had captured the *Active*, a British ship, only to have it claimed by the state of Pennsylvania. Arnold had agreed to use his influence to persuade the state to give up its claim to the ship. In exchange, the sailors promised Arnold half owner-ship of the *Active* and its cargo.

Soon Reed found out that Arnold had also used wagons publicly hired by the state of Pennsylvania to haul cargo he owned from another ship, the *Charming Nancy*, from New Jersey into Philadel-phia.[2] When Reed complained, the Continental Congress appointed a committee to investigate the charges.

In February 1779, Arnold left Philadelphia on a trip to New York. That very day, Reed issued a proclamation on behalf of the state executive coun-cil, making eight charges against Arnold. The proclamation, which was printed in the newspaper and sent to every state, members of Congress, and Washington's headquarters, accused Arnold of: granting passes to people of bad character so that they might take the *Charming Nancy* from Philadelphia to Boston; closing Philadelphia shops in order to buy from them a large amount of foreign goods for himself; requiring militiamen to perform degrading services; illegally purchasing cargo from the captured ship *Active*; using public wagons to transport his private property; illegally helping a Tory woman, Hannah Levy, to cross American lines; being indecent and disrespectful to the state's exec-utive council when it asked him about his use of the state's wagons; and neglecting patriots' needs, while assisting Tories.[3] Until Arnold was removed from office, the proclamation said, the state of Pennsylvania would pay no costs for the army. Furthermore, its militia could be used only in cases of extreme emergency.

The following day, the council ordered the state's attorney general to indict Arnold on the charges. Learning of the charges while en route to New York, Arnold considered returning to Philadelphia. He decided instead to go on to see General Washington at his camp in New Jersey. Washington apparently received him politely but displayed no great warmth. This dismayed Arnold. Washington did, however, express support for Arnold and suggested that he try to outmaneuver the Pennsylvania politicians by seeking a military court-martial rather than a trial by a judge.

On February 16, Congress voted to refer the charges against Arnold to the special congressional committee, chaired by William Paca, that was already investigating Arnold. Only members from Pennsylvania voted against this referral.

Arnold apparently knew committee chairman Paca, who was married to a friend of Peggy's. Arnold went before the committee on March 5 to defend himself. Reed sent no one to make the case against him. The committee voted to clear Arnold of the six charges on which they had the power to decide. They recommended that he be court-martialed by the army on the charges of the misuse of state wagons and militia.

Court-martial

Arnold took the decision as good news. He felt confident that he would be acquitted in a court-martial. In the meantime, he submitted his resignation as military governor of Pennsylvania. Joseph Reed, however, continued to fight. He protested that the Continental Congress had no authority in the matters the committee had considered. He also accused congressmen of secretly trying to overthrow the state constitution of Pennsylvania. As a result of Reed's protests, Congress finally voted to set aside the Paca committee report. Now Congress recommended that Arnold be court-martialed on *four* charges: misusing public wagons, misusing militiamen, making illegal purchases for his own gain from shops ordered closed by the government, and illegally writing passes for Tories.

The court-martial was scheduled for April 30, 1779. On April 24, Reed wrote to General Washington to inform him that, if the army did not find Arnold's use of the wagons a serious offense, the state would never again provide the army with transportation. This was a serious threat. The army could not launch a new offensive without the wagons Pennsylvania could supply.

At the same time, Arnold, too, was writing to Washington. On April 27, Arnold received a note from Washington informing him that his court-martial would be postponed indefinitely. Arnold waited impatiently for further word until May 5. When none arrived, he wrote an emotional plea to Washington for justice:

> Having made every sacrifice of fortune and blood, and become a cripple in the service of my country, I little expected to meet the ungrateful returns I have received from my countrymen; but as Congress have stamped ingratitude as a current coin, I must take it. . . .[4]

The court-martial was rescheduled. Hearings began on December 25, 1779. Finally, on January 26, 1780, the military tribunal issued its verdict. It cleared Arnold of all charges, except that of misusing the state wagons. The tribunal had decided that he had, in fact, intended to pay the teamsters out of his own pocket and that his use of the wagons in no way interfered with their "public service." Nevertheless, his request to use them was "imprudent and improper and . . . it ought not to have been made."[5]

As punishment, Arnold was sentenced to receive a reprimand from George Washington. Following instruction from Congress, Washington wrote Arnold a formal letter of reprimand. Its tone was hardly severe. As historian Richard Boylan wrote, "Washington merely parroted the phrase of the court, refusing to elaborate on what he probably regarded as a minor incident which had been blown up so far out of proportion as to seriously cripple the morale of the already physically crippled Arnold."[6]

Changing Sides

Ironically, by the time Arnold received Washington's gentle scolding, he was actually guilty of a grievous wrong: He was plotting treason. Probably within days of receiving word from Washington that his court-martial would be delayed, Benedict Arnold had contacted Joseph Stansbury, a Philadelphia merchant, with the ultimate aim of abandoning the American cause and joining the British Army.

Peggy Shippen Arnold already knew Stansbury. A Tory when the British Army was in Philadelphia, he had sworn allegiance to the Americans when they arrived to take over the city. Nevertheless, he still corresponded with the British officers he had met in Philadelphia, who were now in New York. Peggy knew this because Stansbury passed cards and letters from some of her friends to these officers. He also placed orders for fancy household goods and finery like hats and fans.[7] So it seems that, when Arnold decided that he wanted to contact the British, it was his wife who suggested that he use Stansbury to deliver his message. Joseph Stansbury later remembered that Arnold sent for him in the spring of 1779. Arnold told Stansbury of "his abhorrence

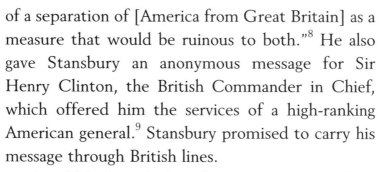

Was Peggy Shippen a Spy, Too?
Benedict Arnold authority William Stanley believes that Peggy Shippen not only encouraged her husband in his treasonous plans but actually committed treason herself. He notes that, in archives in Great Britain, war department files reveal that Peggy Shippen was being paid to spy by the British government when she married Arnold. Revolutionary leaders, however, never found out about her activities as a British informer. Thus she was never arrested or tried for them.

of a separation of [America from Great Britain] as a measure that would be ruinous to both."[8] He also gave Stansbury an anonymous message for Sir Henry Clinton, the British Commander in Chief, which offered him the services of a high-ranking American general.[9] Stansbury promised to carry his message through British lines.

Arnold had made Stansbury promise to tell no one of the letter. Stansbury broke his word, however. In British-occupied New York, he went not to a British officer, but to see an old friend, another Tory named Jonathan Odell. Odell was a minister who was active in British intelligence. Odell arranged a meeting between Stansbury and John André, an old friend of Peggy Shippen's, who was now personal aide to British General Henry Clinton.

Stansbury met André on May 10, 1779.[10] Through Stansbury, André told Arnold that the British were not about to give up the fight against the Americans. Arnold had asked for assurance because he did not want to join a losing team. Stansbury then brought up a matter very important to Arnold: What would the British pay for Arnold's betrayal of the Americans? Although André would not name any specific amount, he did tell Arnold that important military intelligence would be rewarded with "liberality."[11]

By around May 20, Stansbury was back in Philadelphia. There, he met with Arnold, giving him a memo André himself had written. Within a week, Arnold began to send André messages in code, telling him of American battle plans, among other things.[12] In June, André wrote directly to Arnold. He wanted Arnold to secure a new post in the Continental

Benedict Arnold met Major John André (seen here), who would help him betray his country, through his second wife, Peggy Shippen Arnold.

Army and then allow himself and his men to be captured.

At that point, Stansbury informed André that Arnold was upset that the British did not seem more eager to secure his services. Arnold was complaining that André's style was "laconic" and his interest "indifferent."[13] In late July, André wrote to Arnold again, to suggest that they meet. He promised they could then work out the details—the amount the British would pay—concerning Arnold's defection. André went on to say that the British had decided what they really wanted from Arnold: an accurate description of West Point, an important American military fortress on New York's Hudson River.

West Point was very important for the defense of the United States. Although the British Army was based in New York City, as long as American soldiers held West Point, British soldiers from New York and Canada could not easily unite to form a larger and more powerful army.[14]

The Deal

In the months that followed, Arnold tried to get the British to agree to specific terms. He wanted a written guarantee that he would receive ten thousand pounds for his betrayal and another twenty thousand for the surrender of West Point to the British.[15] British command of West Point might well let the

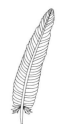

West Point

West Point remained in American hands throughout the revolution, despite Arnold's attempts to transfer it to the British. Afterward, West Point became American government property. In 1802, the United States Military Academy was founded there. Today, West Point is famous as a training college for United States Army officers.

British control the upper Hudson River and split the Continental Army in two.

In August 1779, André wrote to Peggy, offering to send her supplies for making hats. She did not answer him for two months. When she did, she declined his offer. Biographers have speculated that she wanted to convey to him that Arnold was still waiting for guarantees and that, at this time, Arnold was still considering backing out of his agreement with the British. After all, his court-martial had yet to take place. Had Americans risen up and supported him, he might very well have decided to remain loyal to the Continental Army. He could have confessed to Washington the advances he had made to the British, pretending that they were a trick designed to get information from the British about their plans.

Washington had reprimanded Arnold as Congress required. But even after Arnold's court-martial, Washington continued to depend upon him. In the spring of 1780, Washington began to lay plans for a new campaign. He himself would command the center of the army, and Nathanael Greene would take charge of the right wing. Washington wanted to give command of the left wing to Benedict Arnold.[16]

7

TREASON

In April 1780, in a stroke of good fortune for Benedict Arnold, Continental Congressman Philip Schuyler was elected chairman of a committee created to assist General Washington in reorganizing the army. Just days earlier, Arnold had met with Schuyler, who agreed that Arnold deserved command of West Point. As committee chair (and a representative from New York), Schuyler's support for Arnold would carry weight. Arnold was pleased when Schuyler agreed to speak directly with Washington about the appointment.[1]

Arnold Acts

It took longer for the arrangements to be made than Arnold had hoped, however. In June, Schuyler wrote to him, reassuring Arnold of Washington's affection for him and that he was being considered for a new, important post.[2] In the same month, Arnold made a business trip to Connecticut. Before he left, he sent a coded message to his British contacts in New York City, indicating that he expected to be given command of West Point.

While on the trip, Arnold visited West Point. In the company of its then-commander, General Robert Howe, he rode along the batteries erected at riverside and around the seven forts on the hills above.

Arnold then passed descriptions of everything he saw along to the British in another coded message. He told them the works were falling into disrepair, that there were not enough soldiers stationed at West Point, and that Howe had not even stockpiled

After visiting West Point (seen here), Benedict Arnold revealed information about the strategic base to the British.

enough provisions for two weeks.[3] He also spelled out for them specific weak points in the defenses. He pointed out, for example, that a troop of British soldiers could easily take Rocky Point, the most important fort, from behind and then protect it with heavy cannons.

After visiting West Point, Arnold went on to New Haven, Connecticut. He needed to make arrangements to sell his house. He also collected some money owed him. He then returned to Philadelphia. There, he was disappointed to find no message waiting for him from the British. Clinton was, in fact, convinced that Arnold was sincere about his offer to come to the British side. André had been checking to make sure Arnold was telling the truth.

By July 12, Arnold had become very frustrated waiting for word from the British. He sent another message to them. In it, he spelled

British General Henry Clinton (seen here), with the help of his aide John André, made a deal with Arnold to supply them with strategic American plans.

out very precisely the deal he was offering them. He would help the British occupy West Point and capture its garrison in return for twenty thousand pounds.[4]

Finally, toward the end of the month, André wrote back to Arnold. He did not accept Arnold's plan to surrender West Point or agree to Arnold's price outright. However, he did express some interest in Arnold's plan. André also hinted that he would meet Arnold to discuss the matter further.[5]

On July 24, 1780, André met with Clinton. Afterward, he sent Arnold a secret message. It let Arnold know that, once he took command of West Point, a British officer identifying himself as John Anderson would come to settle the deal. André promised Arnold that, if he succeeded in helping the British take West Point, its artillery, stores, and three thousand men, he would be paid the twenty thousand pounds he requested.

By this time, however, Arnold was no longer in Philadelphia to receive André's messages. He was already at West Point, where he planned to meet with General Washington and accept his command. The British messenger had actually delivered André's messages to Peggy, who was unable to have them safely delivered to her husband for almost a month. Arnold would not learn until August 25 that the British had agreed to his terms.

On July 31, 1780, Washington met Arnold at West Point. He did not initially offer him the command of West Point. Instead, he offered Arnold a more important post as the second in command of the entire Continental Army. He wanted Arnold to command half of the American infantry in the field. Arnold said nothing in response. Others who were there remembered that his face became deep red as he listened to Washington's offer.

Arnold and Washington parted for a time, and Arnold rode back to headquarters. When Washington arrived there, they argued over whether Arnold should accept the command Washington offered. Arnold worked hard to convince Washington that his injuries were still too severe to allow him to fight in the field. Although Washington made no decision that day, on August 3 he granted Arnold command of West Point and the area south to Dobbs Ferry.[6] Arnold also received command of a corps of infantry and cavalry.

Treason

Arnold arrived at West Point on August 4, 1780. He moved into what had been General Howe's head-quarters, a house across the river from the forts. In early September, Peggy and their new baby, Edward, made plans to join him there. Hannah Arnold, the sister who had so faithfully cared for his children and his business, did not come with them. Apparently, Arnold had come right out and asked her not to. She, in turn, wrote back to complain about what she called his "ill-natur[ed] letter" and to predict that Peggy would not like living at West Point because of its isolation.[7]

In his new headquarters, Arnold settled down to his new responsibilities. He chose one hundred soldiers to camp around the house to guard the property and run errands for him. He also selected his aides.

Arnold then began to carry out his plans for turning West Point over to Great Britain. He sent many letters to General Washington, complaining about the lack of supplies at West Point, which, he said, prevented him from making repairs. At the same time, he began to order many of the soldiers at West Point to other locations. On August 12, for example, he sent two hundred men out to camps upriver to cut firewood. He sent another two hundred down to Haverstraw to guard an outpost.

On August 30, a man named William Heron came to Arnold to ask for a pass to visit New York City. Heron apparently needed to go there to collect some money. Speaking to Heron in private, Arnold arranged for him to carry a letter to John André. Arnold claimed that he himself had not written this letter.

In New York, Heron began to suspect that something was wrong. He gave the letter to Connecticut Assemblyman Samuel Parsons instead of to André. Parsons assumed that the letter dealt only with business and put it away.[8] Though Heron's suspicions

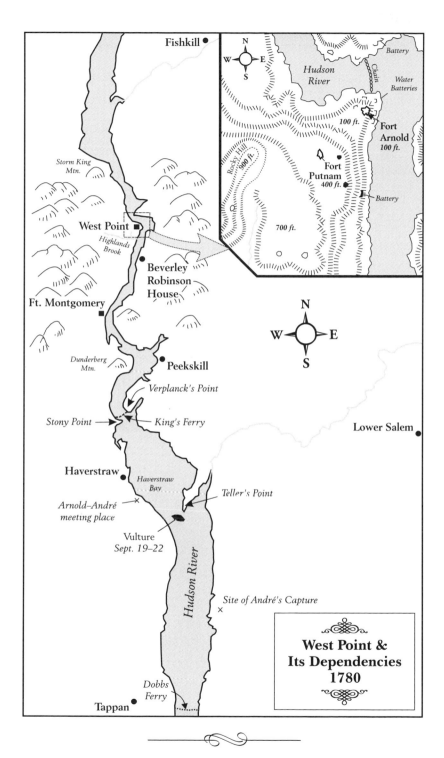

*In 1780, George Washington gave Arnold command of West Point
and the area south to Dobbs Ferry.*

came to nothing, Arnold had been thwarted in his plans to contact André.

On September 3, 1778, Arnold wrote another coded message, to a man named John Anderson—a code name for André. He told his aide about this one. He claimed that Anderson was an American secret agent Arnold hoped could inform him of the enemy's movements. Mary McCarthy, the wife of a British prisoner of war, delivered the message to André.[9]

Missed Meeting

In the meantime, the British were anxious to hear from Arnold and to finalize their plans. On September 9, Arnold received a letter from André, proposing an actual meeting. André wanted to come as a British officer. He said he would pretend to represent a British merchant.[10]

British General Henry Clinton gave André permission to meet Arnold. André waited for Arnold at Dobbs Ferry on September 11. Arnold, too, went to keep this appointment. But as his barge neared the ferry crossing, a British gunboat began to fire upon it. He was forced to retreat to the western shore. André and Colonel Beverley Robinson watched from the eastern side of the river. Finally they all left.[11]

A New Date

On September 15, Arnold wrote to André once again. He had come up with a new plan. He wanted to send a Tory named Joshua Smith to meet André during the night of September 20. Smith would then bring André to Arnold.

The day after sending this message, Arnold received a letter from George Washington. It said that he was on his way to Hartford to meet with French naval officers. Washington planned to stop at Peekskill, New York, on September 17. He needed Arnold to provide him forage for his horses and a guard of fifty soldiers. Washington informed Arnold that he would be traveling secretly. He was counting on Arnold to reveal to no one his mission, route, or timetable. Arnold, however, immediately wrote a letter to André conveying this information. He suggested that this might be a great opportunity for the British to capture Washington, thus winning the war. The British, however, ignored this suggestion.

The Final Arrangements

In the meantime, Peggy and baby Edward had arrived. On September 18, the Arnolds were having dinner with Arnold's aides at the Robinson house. A messenger brought Arnold a letter from Colonel Beverley Robinson, the Tory who owned the house. Robinson was then aboard the *Vulture*, a British sloop of war, out on the Hudson River. Robinson supposedly wanted to meet with Arnold. Arnold had one of his aides write back, refusing his request. Into this official letter, Arnold secretly slipped a message indicating that his messenger would come aboard the *Vulture* on September 20 to meet André. Arnold also wrote a pass for Joshua Smith that would allow him to bring back André, who would be disguised as John Anderson. Smith was never in on the plot—he thought the man using the name "John Anderson" would actually be Colonel Robinson, bringing peace terms from the British to Arnold.

On the other side of the lines, André did his part to prepare for the meeting. He went over the plan with his superior, General Clinton. He seems, however, to have neglected to mention that he would actually be going behind American lines. Later, Clinton said he believed that André and Arnold were planning to meet on neutral territory.

At any rate, Clinton allowed André to go. Legend has it that Clinton then drank a toast to his aide, saying, "Here's to plain John André. May he return Sir John André."[12]

8

CAUGHT!

On September 20, 1779, John André rode to Dobbs Ferry and was taken by boat to the *Vulture*. But Smith never showed up. He had been unable to hire a boatman to take him out to the British sloop. To prevent Robinson and the crew from suspecting the real purpose of his visit, André wrote to Clinton saying he could not return on September 21 because he was ill.

Next, André wrote a letter to Arnold, which Robinson signed. In it, André said that the Americans had violated the code of war a few days earlier by firing on a boat sent out from the *Vulture*. André had made up a reason to contact Arnold to hide the true reason for their correspondence. Arnold received this letter while headed toward the *Vulture*. He had told his men he wanted to inspect his fortifications. Probably he recognized André's handwriting and took it as a sign that André was still on board the *Vulture* and wanted to meet with him.

Arnold rode to Smith's house. Finding that the boatmen once again refused to take Smith out to the *Vulture*, Arnold became extremely angry. He threatened to claim they were British sympathizers and imprison them. Frightened, Samuel and Joseph Colquehoun agreed to row. Arnold wrote a new pass for the Colquehouns and Smith as well as a letter to Robinson in which he pretended to want to meet with him. Carrying these papers, Smith and the Colquehouns set sail. They rowed to the *Vulture* without being stopped.

On board, Smith met with Robinson. Robinson, André, and the ship's commander then conferred. They decided that Arnold's letter to Robinson was just a ploy and that he really wanted to see André.[1]

André had been planning to go ashore in his dress uniform but the captain persuaded him to cover his scarlet jacket with a big blue coat. Robinson then took André out to meet Smith. He introduced him as John Anderson and said Anderson was to meet with Arnold. Smith made no objection. Smith and "Anderson" got in the little boat, which the Colquehouns rowed to the western shore.

André and Arnold Finally Meet

What happened next? The only firsthand accounts of the meeting of Arnold and André that still exist come from Smith. Smith, however, told two different versions of the story, one to an American court when he stood accused of being in league with Arnold, and a second to the British government years later when he wanted payment for the loyalty he claimed to have shown Great Britain.

At any rate, Smith claimed he left "Anderson" waiting on shore and went on foot to a grove of fir trees where Arnold had arranged to meet him. He told Arnold that Robinson had refused to come ashore, sending a representative instead. Arnold pretended to be annoyed but consented to meet with "Anderson," whom Smith then fetched.

André and Arnold then, finally, talked privately for several hours. At 4:00 A.M., Smith came to tell them that the sun would soon rise. Apparently, Arnold and André decided they still had more to talk about, and that André could not yet return to the *Vulture*. They then rode to Smith's house. This placed André in a very dangerous position, well within American lines.

During the early morning, André and Arnold seem to have continued to talk about how the British might best attack West Point. In the meantime, American soldiers shelled the *Vulture*, which moved several hundred yards downstream to get out of the range of the cannon.

Arnold wrote two new passes for André. One granted him permission to go back to the *Vulture.* The other gave him permission to travel overland to Westchester, New York, just in case he could not, for some reason, get back to the sloop.[2] Arnold also gave André papers concerning the Continental Army and West Point, including an analysis of its defects, and a report on its troops.[3]

This is a facsimile reproduction of the pass Arnold gave to André to help him move through enemy lines.

Arnold and André Part

At midmorning, Arnold left for his headquarters. Later, his aides would remember that they had been unhappy that he had spent the night away. They knew he had spent the night at Smith's. But they did not suspect him of treason. Instead, they thought he was making illegal trades with Tories.

André Leaves for British Territory

In the meantime, André remained at Smith's house until nightfall. Stories vary as to why he did not return to the *Vulture*. Historians note that many American vessels appeared on the river after the bombing of the British sloop. At any rate, Smith somehow persuaded André that he could not be rowed out to the *Vulture*. Before setting out, André removed the British uniform he had been wearing under the blue coat. Doing so turned him into a spy—a British officer in disguise behind American lines.

On horseback, Smith and André rode for King's Ferry at Stony Point. There, they boarded the ferry. On the other side of the river, Smith stopped to drink several cups of grog with American Colonel James Livingston, who had fired upon the *Vulture* that morning. André refused to join the party.

Then Smith and André headed south toward White Plains, which lay inside British-held territory. A patrol of American militiamen stopped them and

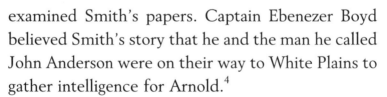

Why Was André Considered a Spy?

John André became a spy—rather than an official emissary of his government—when he broke three rules of war. First, he ventured behind American lines, rather than meeting Arnold in neutral territory. Second, he took papers from Arnold that contained confidential information concerning American military matters. Third, before setting out to return to British territory, André removed the British uniform he had been wearing.

His boss, General Henry Clinton, had specifically warned André against all three actions just before André went to meet Arnold. One can only conclude that André must have realized the risk he was taking.

examined Smith's papers. Captain Ebenezer Boyd believed Smith's story that he and the man he called John Anderson were on their way to White Plains to gather intelligence for Arnold.[4]

André and Smith spent the night at a farmhouse. The next morning, September 23, Smith rode off with André, but left him at Pine's Bridge, which crossed Croton River. On the other side of the bridge, André entered no-man's-land. He should, in essence, have been home free. But then he came to a fork in the road. Instead of choosing the road that led directly to White Plains, he took the wrong road, toward Tarrytown.

André Is Captured

Had André actually reached Tarrytown, all would probably have been well. Many Tories lived there. However, close to town, three bandits—John Paulding, Isaac Van Wart, and David Williams— accosted him. They had been lounging by a stream, playing cards. Seeing him approach, they leapt to their feet and ordered him to stop. Paulding threat- ened him with a musket. Seeing that Paulding wore a British Army coat (which he had stolen from a sol- dier's corpse on a battlefield), André revealed himself as a British Army officer.[5]

At that point, the bandits let André know they were actually on the American side. André showed them his pass from Arnold. Instead of letting him go, however, they made him strip off his clothes. He offered to pay them handsomely to help him make his way to New York. Instead of accepting his bribe, they continued their search of his clothing. In his stockings, they found the papers concerning West Point and General Washington that Arnold had given him.

They took André to American Colonel John Jameson, the commander at North Castle. He examined the papers the bandits had found on André and decided to send André back to Arnold. By the time Jameson made this decision, however, André had already left North Castle, under escort, bound for Arnold's headquarters.

After receiving war plans from Arnold, John André was on his way back to British territory when he was captured by bandits.

But then Major Benjamin Tallmadge arrived at Jameson's. He was an intelligence officer who had been spying for the Continental Army. He told Jameson he had made a mistake by sending André to Arnold. Acting on Tallmadge's advice, Jameson sent soldiers to stop the André party and bring it back. Jameson agreed to send the documents found on André to General George Washington, instead of to Benedict Arnold. Jameson also wrote to Arnold to tell him of "Anderson's" capture.[6]

Now a prisoner in Salem, André himself wrote to Washington on September 24. In the letter, he claimed, "I was involuntarily an impostor."[7] In other words, he claimed he had wanted to continue to wear his uniform but had been persuaded to take it off. He wrote, "I was betrayed . . . into the vile condition of an enemy in disguise within your posts."[8]

The horseman carrying Jameson's message to Arnold left North Castle first. Two hours later, a second horseman started off to deliver Jameson's message to Washington, André's letter, and the incriminating documents in Arnold's handwriting.

The Arnolds Realize They Are in Trouble

Back at Robinson's house, the Arnolds spent Sunday in unhappy company. Smith arrived and told Arnold he had left André at the Croton River. Arnold began to fear for André's safety.

Early on the following morning, Monday, September 25, a messenger arrived to inform Arnold that General Washington was fifteen miles from West Point. He would arrive shortly. Then Colonel Jameson's messenger arrived with the letter informing Arnold of André's capture and the fact that his papers had been sent to Washington. Arnold immediately realized that he would soon be accused of treason.

Arnold received these letters while at the breakfast table. He had read the second without revealing its contents to his companions. Suddenly he rose, excusing himself. He went to his bedroom to speak to his wife.

When he had told her everything, they agreed that he had to try to escape, leaving Peggy and their son behind. He picked up two loaded pistols and some coins and ran for the door. There, he almost ran into David Franks, one of his aides, whom he ordered to have his horse saddled. He told Franks something had happened that required him to leave immediately for West Point. He offered no further detail and said that Franks should explain the situation to Washington when he arrived. Arnold promised he would be back shortly.

Arnold Escapes

Mounting his horse, Arnold took off for the Hudson River. He actually met some members of Washington's party on his way. He asked them to make sure Washington made himself comfortable and ate breakfast at his house. He assured them that he would return soon to confer with Washington. He then galloped to his barge and ordered its oarsmen to take him to Stony Point. Midriver, he saw a rider gallop up to the landing and shout. Arnold ignored him. Then he told the oarsmen to change course, and to take him to the *Vulture*.

Arnold arrived at the *Vulture* under a white flag. After he climbed aboard, Captain Andrew Sutherland and Robinson pumped him for information about André. Arnold turned around to inform the crew of his barge that he had just changed sides and

This is an artist's depiction of Benedict Arnold's escape to New York after his plot to give up West Point was discovered.

was joining the British Army. He asked them to join, too. They refused. Corporal James Larvey shouted, "No sir! One coat is enough for me to wear at one time."[9] This infuriated Arnold. He had Sutherland retain the crew members as prisoners of war.

Arnold had arrived at 11:30 A.M. At three in the afternoon, the *Vulture*, with its new British general—Benedict Arnold—safely on board, set sail for Manhattan, deep in British territory.

9

AFTER ARNOLD'S ESCAPE

George Washington arrived at the Robinson house, where the Arnolds had been living, on September 25, 1780. His men had arrived before him, because he had stopped to examine two earthworks. When Washington arrived, around 10:30 A.M., Major David Franks explained that Arnold had suddenly been called away to West Point. Peggy Shippen Arnold was in her room.

Expecting that Arnold would return in about an hour, Washington and his men sat down to eat. When they finished, they rowed across the river to look at defenses on the west bank. They expected to find Arnold there, but, of course, did not. Washington decided to start inspecting the forts without Arnold.

Everywhere he went, he noticed that the forts had been neglected and that very few men were around.[1] Finally, he returned to the Robinson house about 4:00 P.M.

Peggy Arnold remained out of sight. Yet again, Washington asked where Benedict Arnold was but received no satisfactory reply. Still mystified by his absence, he met Alexander Hamilton, who handed Washington a packet of materials from Lieutenant Colonel John Jameson. These included a letter concerning the capture of "John Anderson" and the papers Anderson (John André) had been carrying.

Going through the documents, Washington recognized Arnold's handwriting on papers conveying confidential information to the British government. Suddenly, Washington began to understand that a man he had trusted had gone over to the enemy. Keeping his realizations to himself for the moment, Washington dined and then called for military aide Richard Varick. Washington informed Varick of Arnold's actions.

Soon a messenger arrived with a message for Washington. Peggy was hysterical at the Robinson house. She was calling frantically for Washington. When Washington appeared at her bedside to comfort her, she accused him of plotting against her and wanting to kill her baby. Unable to calm her down, Washington left.

That evening, he wrote new orders for the protection of West Point. Just before he handed his letters to a messenger, a letter arrived from Arnold. It had been sent ashore from the *Vulture* with a man carrying a flag of truce.

In it, Arnold admitted his treachery, but claimed, "I have ever acted from a principle of love to my country. . . ." He also addressed the matter of his wife, writing:

> I have no favor to ask for myself. I have too often experienced the ingratitude of my country to attempt it; but, from the known humanity of your Excellency, I am induced to ask your protection for Mrs. Arnold from every insult and injury that the mistaken vengeance of my country may expose her to. It ought to fall only on me; she is as good and as innocent as an angel, and is incapable of doing wrong. I beg she may be permitted to return to her friends in Philadelphia, or to come to me, as she may choose. . . .[2]

On September 27, Washington and Alexander Hamilton agreed that Peggy Arnold should be allowed to leave West Point for Philadelphia.[3] On the way, she admitted to a Tory friend that she found faking hysteria very tiring. Her distress had been an act.

Fortification of West Point

Even before the departure of Peggy Arnold, Washington himself worked to strengthen American defenses at West Point. He now reasonably feared a British attack. He sent messages to all available forces. Anthony Wayne's brigade responded with haste, arriving at West Point just four hours after receiving Washington's message.

The Trial of John André

Washington immediately recognized that he could not treat André as a prisoner of war. He had to consider André a spy. Thus, André could receive no special favors. Washington himself never met André. After first being held at the Robinson house, André was moved to a cell at Fort Putnam, overlooking West Point. On September 28, a barge carried André and his guards to Stony Point. From there, they traveled overland to Tappan, where André would be kept under guard in a room in a tavern.

The very next day, an escort marched André to the local church. There, thirteen Continental Army officers listened to his testimony. First, a letter from Washington was read. The board then asked André pointed questions. They wanted to know whether he had come openly as a British soldier or sneaked onto American territory. Claiming he had come under a flag of truce to meet Arnold would have saved his life, because then he would have been considered a prisoner of war and not a spy. However, André told the truth and made no such claim.

After his departure, the board listened to letters from British General Henry Clinton and Benedict Arnold. The letters stated that André had indeed come ashore under a flag of truce and that he had acted under Arnold's orders. Although it seems likely that the board wanted to find André not guilty, its members decided in the long run that André's own testimony had to be believed, rather than the letters. The board, therefore, declared André a spy and sentenced him to death.

The Execution of André

On September 30, General George Washington issued a general order approving the hanging of André and ordered the sentence to be carried out the following day. When André learned of his fate, he reacted calmly. He did, however, write to Washington, pleading to be shot rather than hanged. Death by firing squad, he believed, would be more honorable.

On the day he was sentenced to die, George Washington sent André breakfast. A barber arrived to shave him and style his hair. André arranged his personal items in his trunk and then handed its keys over to his servant.

At the appointed hour, two soldiers escorted him out of the tavern. They started to march up a path lined with soldiers and civilians. Suddenly, André caught sight of the gallows that had been built for him. Later, Ensign Samuel Bowman, one of André's escorts, reported that when André realized he was, in fact, to hang, he exclaimed, "I have borne myself with fortitude but this is too degrading! As respects myself, it is a matter of no consequence, but I have a mother and a sister who will be much mortified by the intelligence."[4]

Nevertheless, he continued to conduct himself with dignity. A horse-drawn cart carrying André's coffin had been drawn up under the gallows. André clambered up onto the coffin. He then paced its length, as he removed his hat and tie. When the hangman came to place the noose around his neck, André prevented him from doing so, preferring to do so himself. He pulled the rope tight and then covered his own eyes with a handkerchief.

Colonel Alexander Scammell, who was in charge of the proceedings, then said André also needed to have his arms tied behind his back. André removed his blindfold to get another handkerchief from his

An artist sketched a view of John André's execution.

pocket. Handing it to the executioner, André then blindfolded himself once again. The hangman tied his arms and then tied the end of the noose to the gallows.

Colonel Scammell asked André if he wanted to make a final statement. All became silent as he replied, "Only that you all bear witness that I die like a soldier and a brave man."[5] With that, Scammell raised his sword and a drum roll commenced. The hangman, back down on the ground, cracked a whip.

A Romantic Hero

Even though André was a spy, many American women found him a very attractive man. After André was hanged and his body was lowered into his coffin, women and girls rushed to cover it with flowers. He was then buried immediately beneath his gallows. Residents of Tappan covered his grave with rocks and stones, to mark it, and planted two cedar trees alongside. A peach tree would grow at its head.[6] Some would say it had been planted from the seed of a fruit given to André by a young girl on his last, sad march. Today, a monument still marks the site of his death in Tappan. On one side it is inscribed with a quotation:

> *He was more unfortunate than criminal*
> *An accomplished man and a gallant officer*
> *—George Washington*[7]

The horses attached to the cart bolted forward, causing André to drop. He died instantly.

Benedict Arnold Enters British Service

Unlike André, Benedict Arnold never had to face a tribunal. He had escaped safely to New York City, where he immediately joined the British Army as a brigadier general of provincial troops. His permanent rank would be that of cavalry colonel. In New York, he learned of the execution of John André. Chief William Smith, who witnessed his reception of the news, recorded in his diary that it left Arnold "vastly disconcerted."[8]

Still, the news scarcely gave him pause. His days were busy. He attended meetings with top-ranking British officers and told them how he thought they might best attack the Americans. He proposed to Henry Clinton that he himself lead an attack on West Point.[9]

In the meantime, he also haggled over what the British Army would pay him for having switched sides. When he met with André, he had been told that he could expect only £6,000 if the plot were discovered. However, he apparently hounded Clinton for £10,000. On October 18, 1780, under Clinton's orders, he received the £6,000 plus an additional £350 for expenses. In today's money, his payoff would be roughly $200,000. Arnold was also promised another £650 a year until he retired from the British Army, at which point he would start to receive an annual pension of £225. The grand total would come to about $400,000 in modern money. (It must be remembered, however, that his change of allegiance also cost him all the property he owned and an enormous amount of back pay he would have received from the Continental Army.)

Arnold's children would also profit from his defection. In November 1780, his eldest son, Benedict, received a commission of his own in the British Army. A year later, his sons Richard, twelve, and Henry, nine, received their own honorary commissions.

Reaction to Arnold's Defection

Many Tories, of course, felt great joy when they learned of Arnold's defection to the British Army. For senior British officers, it seemed of such importance that they had the royal mail delayed until they could write letters telling the news to their superiors on the other side of the Atlantic Ocean. Junior officers would treat Arnold with little respect, however. Some despised him for failing to offer to take André's place before the tribunal.

Americans were outraged at Arnold's actions. Later, Arnold would learn that patriots had decided that, should Arnold ever fall into American hands, his injured left leg would be cut off. The leg would receive a formal military burial, in recognition of the fact that Arnold had been wounded at Quebec, when he was still an American hero. Then, he would be hanged as a spy.

Arnold, however, never had to face much of the Americans' anger. His wife, Peggy, on the other hand, witnessed his effigy (likeness) being burned by an angry mob. Her father had his house ransacked when the Philadelphia sheriff ordered a search for Arnold's papers there.

On October 9, Arnold's appointment as a British general was formally announced. At the same time, the *Royal Gazette* newspaper published a proclamation that Arnold had written concerning his changing of sides. In it, he claimed that he could no longer support the American cause because of the enlistment of French support. On October 27, the fact that Americans could not forgive Arnold for his actions was made abundantly clear when the Philadelphia city council banished Peggy Arnold from the city. She would not be allowed to return for the duration of the war.

Arnold's Legion

One of Arnold's first acts as a British officer was to raise a military unit comprised of Tories and defectors from the American side.[10] Commanding this legion, he led two successful raids against the ports of New London and Groton, Connecticut.[11]

He did relatively little else in the war, however. He suffered so many losses at Fort Griswold in New

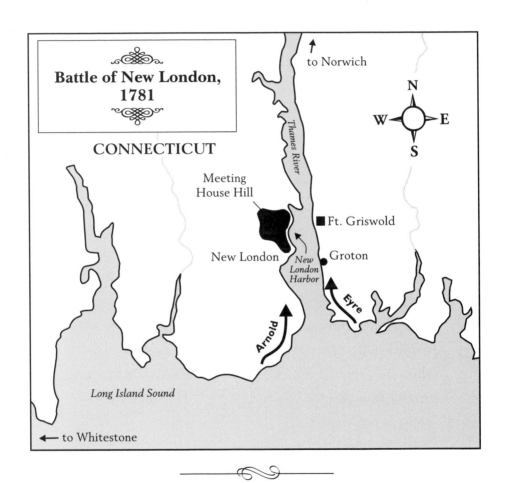

Battle of New London, 1781

CONNECTICUT

to Norwich

N
W   E
S

Thames River

Meeting House Hill

Ft. Griswold

New London

New London Harbor

Groton

Eyre

Arnold

Long Island Sound

to Whitestone

As a British officer Arnold led only two winning battles—in New London and Groton, Connecticut.

London that Clinton never again trusted him to command a large expedition. Arnold's treason, in the long run, did not help the British Army.

After the War

British General Charles Cornwallis surrendered to General George Washington at Yorktown, Virginia, in October 1781. Within weeks, Benedict Arnold and his wife and children—Benedict, Henry, Richard, and Edward—sailed for England, where they would now reside. In London, they received some acclaim. Arnold enjoyed several audiences with King George III. The Prince of Wales was spotted strolling arm-in-arm with Arnold in public gardens. The queen paid attention to Peggy.

However, members of the British Whig party—which had opposed the war—showed contempt for Arnold, whom they openly branded a traitor. Once, when he went to see the House of Commons in session, a member demanded that the bailiff throw Arnold out.

Canada

Soon Arnold's army pay would prove too little to support his family. Peggy still had expensive tastes. After failing in several business ventures, Arnold traveled alone back across the Atlantic to Canada. Just before his departure, Peggy gave birth to a daughter named Sophie.[12] In St. John, New Brunswick,

Arnold founded a shipping and trading company. He also became romantically involved with another woman. In 1786, his illegitimate son, John Sage, was born.[13] The mother's name, however, is no longer known.

At first, Arnold experienced success in his Canadian business ventures. In 1787, he went to England to bring back Peggy and their children Edward, Sophie, and their new son, James. His sister, Hannah, and his son Henry by his first wife, Peggy Mansfield, also came from the United States to live with him. In September 1787, Peggy Shippen Arnold gave birth to a fourth child, whom they named George. But then Arnold's company began to founder. He also suffered in Canada from a reputation as a scoundrel. The Arnolds returned to England, except for Hannah and Henry, who went back to the United States.[14]

After revolutionaries in France beheaded their king, Louis XVI, Great Britain declared war on France. Arnold hoped this would offer him a new opportunity to fight, but the army "viciously snubbed" his offer of services.[15]

He then started a new trading venture, in the West Indies. At the island of St. Kitts, in the Caribbean Sea, he was captured by the French. Ironically, he declared himself to be an American merchant by the name of John Anderson, the same name used earlier by John André. To escape, Arnold bribed French sailors to provide him with a raft, which he then piloted to an English flagship.

For a time, his son Henry joined him in the West Indies, working as his assistant. But Arnold soon sent Henry back to live with his sister, Hannah. He was fond of his son, but believed Henry lacked a head for business.

Benedict Arnold fought for a time for the British Navy in the West Indies. By 1795, he was back in England. Peggy was suffering so severely from cancer that he had to devote considerable time to caring for her. Creditors hounded him. His own health began to fail. By 1801, he suffered terribly from both asthma and gout. His wounded left leg throbbed constantly.

On June 14, 1801, Benedict Arnold died in London, England. He was sixty years old. He had

Benedict Arnold's Grave

A clerk failed to record Benedict Arnold's name correctly in the church's death records when he was buried in London in 1801. When St. Mary's Church underwent renovation around 1900, Arnold's body was disinterred and reburied in an unmarked grave along with hundreds of others. Today, there is a monument at St. Mary's that announces the fact that he is buried there.

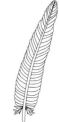

become a poor, miserable man, who lacked honor and respect. A week after his death, he was buried. Less than one hundred mourners attended his funeral. Four state carriages brought dignitaries and seven mourning coaches carried other friends and family members to the church of St. Mary's, Battersea, in an unfashionable London neighborhood south of the Thames River. There was no cannon salute. Arnold did not receive the military honors he had hoped the British Army would pay him.

Newspapers did report Arnold's death, but they devoted little room to it. Some of what was written about him after he died was very unkind, even in Great Britain. The London *Post* pointed out he had died "without notice, a sorry reflection [thought] this for . . . other turncoats. . . ."[16]

10

LEGACY

Following the death of her husband, Peggy Shippen Arnold suffered a number of unhappy surprises. In his will, Benedict Arnold provided land and money for education and income to his illegitimate son, John Sage, in Canada. It is unclear whether Peggy already knew of Sage's existence. Arnold also left bequests for all his other children and Hannah. But there was not enough money in his estate for the bequests to be paid.[1] Peggy ended up with huge debts. The house Arnold had given her as a wedding present turned out to be owned by someone else. She was forced to move out of their mansion in London into a far smaller dwelling, to sell her

furniture, and to do without luxuries such as wine and new clothes.

Peggy did receive the royal pension that the British government had awarded Arnold for his military service. This pension and sales of goods and bank stock allowed her to pay off Arnold's debts, which totaled around £6,000, an enormous sum, within two years. She sent the money Benedict Arnold had bequeathed to his three sons by his first marriage and to Hannah.[2] (By this time, they were all living with John Sage in Canada.[3]) She also recovered enough financially to send her children to good schools and to purchase a commission in the army for their son William.

She herself probably never again enjoyed a very comfortable life. Peggy Shippen Arnold died of uterine cancer on August 24, 1804, at the age of forty-four, just three years after her husband's death and one year after discharging his debts.

Arnold's Reputation Today

Since his death, Benedict Arnold has remained one of the most enigmatic characters in American history. Today, he remains someone whom virtually all Americans seem to have heard of, even if all they know is that he betrayed his country. Indeed, his name has entered the English language as a synonym for "traitor."

Scholars continue to study Arnold, precisely because of his mysterious character. He has been the

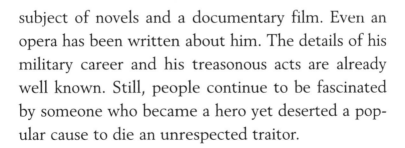

Other Traitors

Benedict Arnold may well be the most famous traitor in American history. However, he is not the only one. During the American Revolution, several other colonists were accused of treason, convicted, and hanged. They had recruited men for the British Army or furnished the British with supplies.

Other traitors came after the revolution. Aaron Burr's was the most famous treason trial held in the United States in the nineteenth century. He was accused of trying to break up the United States, allowing both Spain and Great Britain to reclaim territory.

Only two Americans have ever been convicted and executed for treason in peacetime. They were Julius and Ethel Rosenberg, who were convicted of selling secrets concerning atomic weapons to a Soviet spy in 1951. They were executed in 1953.

subject of novels and a documentary film. Even an opera has been written about him. The details of his military career and his treasonous acts are already well known. Still, people continue to be fascinated by someone who became a hero yet deserted a popular cause to die an unrespected traitor.

Why Did Arnold Do It?

After he had become a traitor, Arnold publicly stated that he had done so because he was extremely unhappy with the military alliance the United States had made with France. He believed this alliance would make it impossible for Americans to win the war.

In reality, however, he seems to have deserted the American side for two reasons: First, he felt unappreciated by the American people. He had been a hero several times during the war. Yet many times he had been accused of wrongdoing. Regardless of whether these accusations were true, he resented them because they prevented him from getting the honor he felt he deserved. Ever since his father had died as a disrespected town drunk, Arnold had sought to restore the honor and respect the family had once enjoyed. Throughout his career, however, he never seemed to succeed in this goal. Perhaps he hoped he could earn this respect from the British through his defection.

Another reason he may have committed treason is because of his bad leg. He knew he could no longer fight in the field. He no longer had the stamina, and he was in constant pain. Some historians have speculated that he wanted to find a new way to feel like a hero. After changing sides, he expected the British to praise him lavishly.

Nevertheless, the most obvious reason he became a traitor was for the money. Throughout the war, he had spent much of his own fortune. He had begun to think that he would never be paid in full for his services and expenses while in the Continental

Benedict Arnold, in recent years, has become more respected for his brilliant career as a general. However, he is usually better remembered for betraying his country.

Army. So when the British agreed to pay him a large amount of money for his betrayal, he readily agreed. Both he and his wife wanted to live their lives in luxury. As one of his contemporaries, Continental Army Colonel John Brown, said of Arnold even before the world learned of his treason, "Money is this man's god, and to get enough of it he would sacrifice his country."[4]

Chronology

1741—Benedict Arnold is born on January 14.

1742—Benedict's sister Hannah is born.

1752—Arnold goes away to school.

1754—Returns home; Apprenticed to the Lathrops as an apothecary.

1757—Accompanies militiamen marching to fight the Mohawk.

1759—Mother, Hannah King Arnold, dies.

1761—Father dies.

1762—Arnold completes his apprenticeship; Opens his own shop in New Haven.

1763—Buys back the family estate in Norwich.

1764—Sells the estate for a profit; His sister, Hannah, moves to New Haven to live with him.

1766—In January, accused of smuggling, Arnold is ordered to pay fine for disturbing the peace.

1767—Marries Peggy Mansfield in New Haven.

1775—*January*: Joins the Fort Guards.

April 19: Battles of Lexington and Concord take place.

May 10: With Ethan Allen, leads American troops in taking Fort Ticonderoga.

May 12: The Green Mountain Boys take Crown Point, another fortification on Lake Champlain.

June 19: Wife, Peggy Mansfield Arnold, dies.

July: Arnold meets with American General Philip Schuyler in Albany, New York, to discuss further campaign plans.

September: Arnold leaves Massachusetts with eleven hundred soldiers to cross the Maine wilderness and attack Quebec.

December 2: Arnold and Montgomery and their troops begin a siege of Quebec.

December 30: Injured in an assault on Quebec.

1776—*Summer*: Arnold builds a fleet of boats for the Americans to fight with in Canada.

October 11–13: Arnold's fleet loses Battle of Valcour Island.

1777—*September 19*: Fights in the first Battle of Saratoga.

October 7: Distinguishes himself in the second Battle of Saratoga.

1778—*May*: Becomes military governor of Philadelphia.

1779—*February*: Charged with abusing power as military governor; Resigns office.

April 8: Marries Peggy Shippen.

May: Arnold contacts the British for the first time, offering to change sides.

1780—*January 26*: Court-martial ends; Receives a gentle reprimand from Washington, his sole punishment.

July: Washington gives Arnold command of West Point.

September 21–22: Arnold and André meet to discuss plans for Arnold to hand West Point over to the British.

September 23: André is captured.

September 25: Flees and joins the British Army.

October 2: John André is hanged.

1781—*Fall*: The Arnold family moves to England.

1801—*June 14*: Dies in London.

CHAPTER NOTES

Chapter 1. The Battle of Ticonderoga

1. Thomas Fleming, *Liberty! The American Revolution* (New York: Viking Penguin, 1997), p. 133.

2. Clare Brandt, *The Man in the Mirror: A Life of Benedict Arnold* (New York: Random House, 1994), p. 22.

3. Frank Northern Magill, *Great Lives from History, American Series* (Pasadena, Calif.: Salem Press, 1987), vol. 1, p. 86.

4. James Kirby Martin, *Benedict Arnold: Revolutionary Hero* (New York: New York University Press, 1997), p. 65.

5. Willard M. Wallace, "Benedict Arnold: Traitorous Patriot," *George Washington's Generals and Opponents: Their Exploits and Leadership*, ed. George Athan Billias (New York: Da Capo Press, 1994), p. 166.

6. Martin, p. 67.

7. Brandt, pp. 26–27.

8. Ibid., p. 27.

9. Martin, p. 71.

10. Brandt, p. 27.

Chapter 2. The Early Years

1. William Stanley, "General Benedict Arnold," Norwich *History and Genealogical Information*, <http://www.norwich.org/nhistory.html> (January 27, 1999).

2. Clare Brandt, *The Man in the Mirror: A Life of Benedict Arnold* (New York: Random House, 1994), p. 3; James Kirby Martin, *Benedict Arnold: Revolutionary Hero* (New York: New York University Press, 1997), p. 15.

3. Martin, p. 17.

4. Ibid.; Brandt, p. 4.

5. Brandt, pp. 5–6.

6. Willard M. Wallace, "Benedict Arnold: Traitorous Patriot," *George Washington's Generals and Opponents: Their Exploits and Leadership*, ed. George Athan Billias (New York: Da Capo Press, 1994), p. 165.

7. Brandt, p. 4.

8. Stanley, <http://www.norwich.org/nhistory.html>.

9. Martin, p. 21.

10. Wallace, p. 164.

11. Martin, p. 26.

12. Brandt, p. 6.

13. Wallace, p. 164.

14. Brandt, p. 7.

15. Ibid., p. 6.

16. Martin, pp. 30–31.

17. Ibid., p. 31.

18. Ibid., pp. 29, 444.

19. Ibid., p. 29.

20. Ibid., p. 36.

21. Ibid., p. 37.

22. Benedict Arnold to Dr. William Jepson, New Haven, December 6, 1763.

23. Martin, pp. 52–53.

24. Brandt, pp. 11–12.

Chapter 3. Arnold Becomes a Rebel

1. Brian Richard Boylan, *Benedict Arnold: The Dark Eagle* (New York: W. W. Norton & Company, 1973), p. 38.

2. James Kirby Martin, *Benedict Arnold: Revolutionary Hero* (New York: New York University Press, 1997), p. 43.

3. Ibid.

4. Boylan, p. 39.

5. Martin, p. 44.

6. William Stanley, "General Benedict Arnold," *Norwich History and Genealogical Information*, <http://www.norwich.org/nhistory.html> (January 27, 1999).

7. Clare Brandt, *The Man in the Mirror: A Life of Benedict Arnold* (New York: Random House, 1994), pp. 14, 15, 16.

8. Ibid., pp. 14–15.

9. Ibid., pp. 16–17.

10. Benson Bobrick, *Angel in the Whirlwind: The Triumph of the American Revolution* (New York: Simon & Schuster, 1997), p. 135.

11. Boylan, p. 39.

12. Bobrick, pp. 135, 136.

13. Martin, p. 62.

14. Ibid., p. 63.

15. Thomas Fleming, *Liberty! The American Revolution* (New York: Viking Penguin, 1997), p. 130.

16. Martin, p. 73.

17. Bobrick, p. 139.

18. Martin, p. 93.

19. Ibid., p. 94.

20. Douglas Southall Freeman, *Washington* (Norwalk, Conn.: The Easton Press, 1968), p. 236.

21. Martin, p. 99.

22. Brandt, p. 38.

23. Ibid., p. 39.

24. Martin, p. 106.

25. Freeman, p. 238.

26. Martin, p. 107.

27. Ibid., p. 109.

28. Ibid., p. 114.

Chapter 4. Quebec and Saratoga

1. Quoted in James Kirby Martin, *Benedict Arnold: Revolutionary Hero* (New York: New York University Press, 1997), pp. 102, 461.

2. Douglas Southall Freeman, *George Washington: A Biography* (New York: Charles Scribner's Sons, 1948–1957), vol. 3, p. 538.

3. Martin, p. 120.

4. Ibid., p. 124.

5. Ibid., p. 131.

6. Ibid., p. 134.

7. Ibid., p. 140.

8. Benson Bobrick, *Angel in the Whirlwind: The Triumph of the American Revolution* (New York: Simon & Schuster, 1997), p. 170.

9. Ibid., p. 173.

10. Brian Richard Boylan, *Benedict Arnold: The Dark Eagle* (New York: W.W. Norton & Company, 1973), p. 68.

11. Ibid., p. 70.

12. Martin, p. 226.

13. Bobrick, p. 274.

14. Ibid., p. 280.

15. William Stanley, "General Benedict Arnold" *Norwich History and Genealogical Information*, <http://www.norwich.org/nhistory.html>.

16. Martin, p. 426.

Chapter 5. Philadelphia and Peggy Shippen

1. James Thomas Flexner, *The Traitor and the Spy: Benedict Arnold and John André*, 2nd ed. (Boston: Little, Brown and Company, 1975), p. 221.

2. James Kirby Martin, *Benedict Arnold: Revolutionary Hero* (New York: New York University Press, 1997), p. 426.

3. Clare Brandt, *The Man in the Mirror: A Life of Benedict Arnold* (New York: Random House, 1994), p. 149.

4. Willard M. Wallace, "Benedict Arnold: Traitorous Patriot," *George Washington's Generals and Opponents: Their Exploits and Leadership*, ed. George Athan Billias (New York: Da Capo Press, 1994), p. 184.

5. Brian Richard Boylan, *Benedict Arnold: The Dark Eagle* (New York: W.W. Norton & Company, 1973), p. 157.

6. Brandt, p. 149.

Chapter 6. Changing Sides

1. Quoted in Benson Bobrick, *Angel in the Whirlwind: The Triumph of the American Revolution* (New York: Simon & Schuster, 1997), p. 410.

2. Clare Brandt, *The Man in the Mirror: A Life of Benedict Arnold* (New York: Random House, 1994), pp. 155, 161, 170.

3. Ibid., p. 170.

4. James Thomas Flexner, *The Traitor and the Spy: Benedict Arnold and John André*, 2nd ed. (Boston: Little, Brown and Company, 1975), p. 277.

5. Brian Richard Boylan, *Benedict Arnold: The Dark Eagle* (New York: W. W. Norton & Company, 1973), p. 161.

6. Ibid., p. 162.

7. Flexner, p. 276.

8. Ibid.

9. Ibid.

10. Brandt, p. 177.

11. Ibid., p. 178.

12. Ibid., p. 179.

13. Boylan, p. 178.

14. Brandt, p. 189.

15. Boylan, p. 181.

16. Ibid., p. 183.

Chapter 7. Treason

1. James Thomas Flexner, *The Traitor and the Spy: Benedict Arnold and John Andre*, 2nd ed. (Boston: Little, Brown and Company, 1975), p. 307.

2. Benson Bobrick, *Angel in the Whirlwind: the Triumph of the American Revolution* (New York: Simon & Schuster, 1997), p. 414.

3. Ibid.

4. Ibid., p. 182.

5. Ibid.

6. Flexner, p. 317.

7. Brandt, p. 204.

8. Ibid., pp. 209, 211.

9. Ibid., p. 209.

10. Ibid., p. 210.

11. Ibid., p. 211.

12. Brian Richard Boylan, *Benedict Arnold: The Dark Eagle* (New York: W. W. Norton & Company, 1973), p. 195.

Chapter 8. Caught!

1. Brian Richard Boylan, *Benedict Arnold: The Dark Eagle* (New York: W. W. Norton & Company, 1973), pp. 198, 200.

2. Ibid., p. 204.

3. Clare Brandt, *The Man in the Mirror: A Life of Benedict Arnold* (New York: Random House, 1994), p. 218.

4. Boylan, p. 207.

5. Ibid., p. 210.

6. Ibid., p. 211.

7. Ibid., p. 213.

8. Ibid.

9. Ibid., p. 219.

Chapter 9. After Arnold's Escape

1. Douglas Southall Freeman, *George Washington: A Biography* (New York: Charles Scribner's Sons, 1948–1957), vol. 5, p. 198.

2. Ibid., p. 203.

3. Ibid., p. 209.

4. Brian Richard Boylan, *Benedict Arnold: The Dark Eagle* (New York: W. W. Norton & Company, 1973), p. 234.

5. Ibid., pp. 235–236.

6. Ibid., p. 248.

7. Ibid., p. 253.

8. Quoted in James Thomas Flexner, *The Traitor and the Spy: Benedict Arnold and John André*, 2nd ed. (Boston: Little, Brown and Company, 1975), p. 394.

9. Flexner, p. 397.

10. Boylan, p. 239.

11. Ibid., p. 240.

12. Clare Brandt, *The Man in the Mirror: A Life of Benedict Arnold* (New York: Random House, 1994), p. 261.

13. Ibid.

14. Ibid., pp. 261–263, 269.

15. Boylan, p. 243.

16. Brandt, p. 275.

Chapter 10. Legacy

1. Clare Brandt, *The Man in the Mirror: A Life of Benedict Arnold* (New York: Random House, 1994), p. 275.

2. Ibid., p. 277.

3. Ibid., p. 275.

4. Quoted in Benson Bobrick, *Angel in the Whirlwind: The Triumph of the American Revolution* (New York: Simon & Schuster, 1997), p. 405.

GLOSSARY

apprentice—A person who enters into a contract under which he or she works for no pay for a specified period of time for an artisan or craftsman, who in turn teaches him or her a trade.

barracks—Sleeping quarters for military personnel.

colony—Territory settled by emigrants from a distant country and governed by the parent country.

contraband—Goods that law has declared it illegal to import or export.

court-martial—A military trial, presided over by a military tribunal, that determines the guilt or innocence and punishment given to a soldier or sailor accused of breaking military law.

effigy—A dummy representing a hated person.

gout—A painful disease in which the joints become inflamed because of uric acid deposits.

militia—A military company made up of volunteers, rather than professional soldiers.

privateer—A ship that a private individual owns and commands during wartime, which the government has authorized to attack and capture enemy ships.

siege—The surrounding of a town or city by soldiers attempting to capture it or force it to surrender.

sloop—A sailing ship or boat with only one mast and rigging at fore and aft that features just one headsail.

traitor—A person who betrays his or her country.

treason—Betrayal of one's country.

wicket—A small gate or door.

FURTHER READING

Books

Bobrick, Benson. *Angel in the Whirlwind: The Triumph of the American Revolution.* New York: Simon & Schuster, 1997.

Dolan, Edward F. *The American Revolution: How We Fought the War for Independence.* Brookfield, Conn.: Millbrook Press, 1995.

Fleming, Thomas. *Liberty! The American Revolution.* New York: Viking, 1997.

Kent, Deborah. *The American Revolution: "Give Me Liberty, or Give Me Death!"* Hillside, N.J.: Enslow Publishers, Inc., 1994.

Martin, James Kirby. *Benedict Arnold: Revolutionary Hero.* New York: New York University Press, 1997.

Rinaldi, Ann. *Finishing Becca: A Story about Peggy Shippen and Benedict Arnold.* San Diego, Calif.: Harcourt, 1994.

Internet Addresses

Henretta, James. "The Enigma of Benedict Arnold." *The Early America Review.* 1997. <http://www.earlyamerica.com/review/fall97/arnold.html> (May 17, 2000).

Independence Hall Association. "Who Served Here? Benedict Arnold." *Historic Valley Forge.* 1998–2000. <http://www.ushistory.org/valleyforge/served/arnold.html> (May 17, 2000).

PBS Online. "Benedict Arnold's Leg." *Liberty!* 1997. <http://www.pbs.org/ktca/liberty/chronicle/ben.arnold.leg.html> (May 17, 2000).

INDEX